FOLLOW ME

DAVID PLATT

Published by LifeWay Press®
© 2013 David Platt
Reprinted November 2013

ISBN 9-7814-3002-5498
Item 005588672

Dewey decimal classification: 248.83
Subject headings: ADOLESCENCE \ DISCIPLESHIP \
CHRISTIAN LIFE

All Scripture quotations are taken from the Holman Christian
Standard Bible®, Copyright © 1999, 2000, 2002, 2003, 2009
by Holman Bible Publishers. Used by permission. Holman
Christian Standard Bible®, Holman CSB®, and HCSB® are
federally registered trademarks of Holman Bible Publishers.

Photo of David Platt: Allison Lewis

To order additional copies of this resource, write to LifeWay
Church Resources Customer Service; One LifeWay Plaza;
Nashville, TN 37234-0113; fax (615) 251-5933; phone toll
free (800) 458-2772; order online at www.lifeway.com; e-mail
orderentry@lifeway.com; or visit the LifeWay Christian Store
serving you.

Printed in the United States of America

Kids Ministry Publishing
LifeWay Church Resources
One LifeWay Plaza
Nashville, TN 37234-0172

CONTENTS

- **What does it mean to be *born again*?**

Nicodemus knew the religious world. However, he noticed something different about Jesus. He wanted to know what it meant to be a follower of Jesus.

- **Why are you interested in becoming a follower of Jesus?**

THINK ABOUT THIS

Many people have been taught that becoming a follower of Jesus only requires believing certain truths or saying specific words. This is not true. Jesus is worth more than intellectual belief (things that you believe in your head, but do not live out in your life). Following Jesus means more than repeating a prayer after someone. Becoming a Christian is more than a feeling. Following Jesus means giving up yourself so Jesus can live in and through you—all the time. Reread that last sentence. Now underline it. Did you get the message? Being a Christian means Jesus lives in YOU.

You may be wondering, *How does a person become a Christian*? Read these three statements. Circle the statement(s) that are in the Bible.

Ask Jesus into your heart.

Invite Jesus into your life.

Pray this prayer after me, and you will be saved.

Which one(s) did you circle? Would it surprise you to know NONE of these statements is in the Bible? Nowhere in the Bible is anyone ever told to ask Jesus into his life. That may surprise you and make you wonder, *Then how does a person become a Christian*? I will address this, but before I do, respond to this question.

- **Can a person know about Jesus yet not know Jesus? Why or why not?**

Think about your answer. Let me ask you some more questions to help you better understand.

- **Who is your favorite television star, athlete, or singer?**

- **What do you know about the person?**

- **How did you learn this information?**

- **If this person walked into a restaurant where you were eating, would you recognize him? Would he know you?**

- **When was the last time you really spent time getting to know him, learning what he likes and does not like?**

The truth is most of us know a lot about people, but we do not personally know them. We can have head knowledge of a person without having a close friendship. The same thing happens with many people and Jesus. Read Jesus' words recorded in Matthew 7:21-23.

deny

to disown

- **What did Jesus say would happen to people who are not His followers?**

Jesus calls His followers to the "narrow way." Throughout His life, Jesus taught the way His followers should live. He warned them of things that would happen to them because they were His followers. Read what Jesus said to His disciples in Matthew 16:24-25.

- **What does it mean to *deny yourself*?**

- **In what ways do you deny yourself?**

- **What does it mean to *take up your cross and follow Jesus*?**

- **What does it mean to *leave everything behind*?**

Shortly before Jesus was crucified, He told His disciples they would be persecuted (to be treated in a cruel way) and put to death, hated by all the people because of Him. (At the end of this week, you will learn what tradition says happened to several of Jesus' followers.) These men were willing to leave everything behind and follow Jesus. Leaving everything behind means the disciples were willing to leave their homes, families, friends, jobs, and everything they owned to follow Jesus.

Throughout the Gospels (Matthew, Mark, Luke, and John), Jesus' message is clear. To follow Jesus means to die—to die to self. Does this scare you? Are you willing to do this? Following Jesus involves losing your life … and finding new life in Him. Take a few minutes and pray. Tell God how you feel about what you just read. Be honest! (He already knows.)

Yesterday we started a discussion about becoming a follower of Jesus. Let's continue our discussion today.

SEARCH THE SCRIPTURES

Read Matthew 7:21.

- **What did Jesus say about the people who would enter heaven?**

- **What does it mean to *do the will of the Father*?**

THINK ABOUT THIS

Some people would say doing the will of the Father means doing good things and working to earn salvation. That is not what Matthew 7:21 says. Jesus was not saying that a person's works are what allows him to receive salvation. God's grace is the only basis for salvation. Jesus taught that only people who are obedient to God will enter heaven. When a person becomes a Christian, her life should reflect her relationship of following Jesus. God is calling us to follow Jesus—to do more than just know about Him. God wants us to be different because of the difference Jesus makes in our lives.

Let's examine how a person becomes a Christian. Read "God's Plan" (pages 23-24).

Are you a Christian? Take a few minutes to thank God for the gift of salvation He provided you. Ask God to help you become a completely sold-out, follower of Jesus.

If you are not a Christian, take a few minutes and talk with your pastor, Bible study leader, or parent about Jesus. Jesus wants to be your Savior and Lord, but only He can do the work of changing your life through His Holy Spirit.

REPENTANCE

If you had to write down one word to summarize everything Jesus taught, what word would you write?

The word that best describes Jesus' teaching is REPENT. Read the definition of *repent*. When people repent, they turn from one direction to the opposite. From that point forward, they think differently, believe differently, feel differently, love differently, and live differently.

> ## repent
> to feel sorry for your sins and make up your mind to do what is right; to change

Jesus' call to repentance is a call for people to turn away from their sin and dependence on themselves for salvation. We can only be saved by turning from our sin and ourself, and turning toward Jesus.

When you become a follower of Jesus, everything changes.

You realize who God is, what Jesus has done, and how much you need Him.

Your desires change.

You love the same things God loves.

You want the same things He wants.

Your will changes.

You go wherever God says go.

You do whatever He says do.

Your reason for living changes.

You live to honor and glorify God.

Jesus will do some amazing things in your life if you are willing and obedient to Him. Are you willing to be a follower of Jesus? Be careful how you respond.

Think about Simon Peter, Andrew, James, and John as they walked with Jesus along the Sea of Galilee. Do you think these men knew how their lives were going to change when they left their fishing businesses to follow Jesus?

- **In what ways has your life changed since you began following Jesus?**

- **In which areas of your life do you most see the need for on-going change?**

- **Are you willing for Jesus to change these areas? If so, tell Him right now.**

►SEARCH THE SCRIPTURES

Read Galatians 4:4-5 and Ephesians 1:5. What do these verses tell you about your relationship with God? Throughout Scripture, God uses the picture of adoption to describe His relationship with His people.

Read "Caleb's Story."

Caleb's Story

RUSSIA

KAZAKHSTAN

CHINA

My wife Heather and I felt God leading us to adopt. We began by trying to decide where in the world God was leading us to adopt a child. God led us to the country of Kazakhstan (kah-zahk-stahn). After completing all the government forms, home studies, physicals, and fingerprints, we were ready for our child. We waited and waited. Every day we would think about our child. We did not know if our child was a boy or a girl. We could not wait until the day we held our child in our arms.

Finally, about a year later, I received an e-mail with a picture of a boy. He was nine months old. His parents abandoned him at birth. The baby was in need of a home—a mom and dad. I printed the picture and showed it to Heather. We laughed, we cried, we rejoiced, and within two weeks, we were on a plane to Kazakhstan.

On February 15, 2006, we arrived in Kazakhstan and were taken to the orphanage. A woman came around the corner with a baby in her arms. I cannot describe the feelings I had at that moment. The woman handed the baby to us, and for the first time, Caleb looked into the eyes of a mom and dad.

We stayed in Kazakhstan for four months, visiting Caleb. We held him, fed him, sang to him, laughed with him, and crawled all over the floor with him. Finally, the day came for us to adopt him. We were told what to wear, what to say, and how to act when we stood before the judge. Our hearts were pounding as the events took place. After a number of questions and testimonies about Caleb's background, the judge said, "I give permission for this adoption. This child now belongs to David and Heather Platt." My wife and I left the room crying. We were ready to pick up Caleb and bring him home with us.

Caleb's adoption reminds me of the relationship God wants to have with us. Caleb did not look for a mom and dad. My wife and I started the process of adopting him. In the same way, God began the process of adopting us into His family. We do not become God's children because of anything we do. God does not provide salvation because of something we do. Instead, before we were even born, God was working to adopt us.

► THINK ABOUT THIS

Think about your life. When did God begin the process of adopting you into His family? Circle the answer you think best answers the question.

Before you were born

At your birth

When you were five years old

Did you circle the first answer? Read Psalm 139:13. Before you were born, God put your body together. He created you and made it possible for Him to adopt you into His family.

- **How does it make you feel to know God loves you so much that He wants you to be a part of His family?**

- **Caleb's life was different after being adopted. In what ways is your life different since becoming a part of God's family?**

Spend time telling God how you feel about being adopted into His family. Thank Him for beginning the process of adopting you, even before you were born.

Have you ever heard someone say, "It was just a little white lie"? Does that mean it was not a lie? Anything that is not true is a lie! In the same way, anything that goes against what God says and wants is a sin. God calls a sin—SIN! Period.

SEARCH THE SCRIPTURES

Read Romans 3:23 and Romans 6:23. What do these verses say about sin?

Read "Azeem's Story."

Azeem's Story

Azeem, an Arab Christian, was sharing the gospel with a taxi driver in his Muslim country. The driver believed that he would pay for his sin for a little while in hell, but then he would surely go to heaven after that. After all, he had not done too many bad things.

Azeem said to the driver, "If I slapped you in the face, what would you do to me?"

The driver said, "I would throw you out of my taxi."

Azeem continued, "If I went up to a stranger on the street and slapped him on the face, what would he do to me?"

The driver said, "He would probably call his friends and beat you up."

Azeem asked, "What if I went to a policeman and slapped him on the face? What would he do?"

"You would be beat up for sure, and then thrown into jail," the driver responded.

Finally, Azeem asked, "What if I went to the king of this country, and I slapped him in the face? What would happen to me then?"

The driver looked at Azeem and laughed. He said, "You would die."

- **How did the consequences of the man's actions change as the person being slapped changed?**

Let's apply this story to our relationship with God. Many people think they can do something that will not really affect them. For example, a preteen may think, *I can steal a piece of gum. No one will miss a small piece of gum.* Next the preteen thinks, *I can cheat on my science test.* He says, "It is not hurting anyone." The preteen continues to do things that he does not think will really impact him. Soon, the preteen is using God's name in inappropriate ways. What does God think about the preteen's actions? Is stealing gum wrong? Is cheating on a test wrong? Is using God's name in inappropriate ways wrong? Are these sins?

The answer to these questions is YES! Stealing, cheating, and using God's name in inappropriate ways are sins. God does not grade sin as "small," "medium," and "large." Unlike the taxi driver who thought the consequences would change depending on who was being slapped, in God's eyes a sin is a sin, no matter how big or small.

- **How serious is your sin? Whether you lied, cheated, stole, or spoke God's name in an inappropriate way, you sinned.**

THINK ABOUT THIS

Check out these Bible verses related to sin. Write down a few words to help you remember what you read about sin.

John 8:34

John 3:20

Romans 1:28

Ephesians 4:18

1 Peter 2:11

grace
undeserved love given to people by God

So, is there any hope for us? Yes, this is where God's grace impacts our lives. God wants to have a relationship with us. Do you remember how Jesus invited Simon Peter, Andrew, James, and John to follow Him? Jesus was not drawn to these men nor did He call them because of who they were in the world's view, but because of who they were in His view. These men did not have many things in their favor. They were not the wealthiest or the best educated men, and they were probably not well respected. They were probably not men most people would invite to join them for anything. But that was Jesus' point. These men did not deserve the invitation to follow Jesus, yet He invited them. Later, Jesus told the men, "You did not choose Me, but I chose you" (John 15:16).

- **Think about your own life. Why do you desire to follow Jesus?**

- How do you respond when you get invited to a friend's house?

- Do you look forward to the visit? Why or why not?

- How would you respond if you were invited to the White House?

I remember the first invitation I received from the White House. When I saw the e-mail titled "From the Office of the President of the United States," I began to wonder if this was a joke or if the invitation was real. I opened the e-mail and read, "The President requests the pleasure of your company at the White House." I did some research and discovered the e-mail was real! I had been invited to the White House. I canceled all my appointments on the day I was to be in Washington. I was honored to have been invited to meet the President.

If this is how I responded when the President invited me to meet him, how should I feel when God invites me to spend time with Him?

Once again read Jesus' invitation to Simon Peter, Andrew, James, and John (Matthew 4:18-22).

- **How did Simon Peter, Andrew, James, and John respond to Jesus' invitation?**

Jesus is not some puny religious teacher begging for people to follow Him. He is the all-sovereign Lord who deserves submission from everyone. Do you understand the opportunity Jesus is giving you to follow Him? Jesus' invitation includes more than church attendance or being a part of a church group. Jesus' invitation to follow Him means committing your life (EVERYTHING) to Him.

submission
volunteering to follow another person and do what he or she wants to be done

Think about these areas of your life. Rate how committed you are in each area.

Very Committed_____Not Committed

School

Very Committed_____Not Committed

Sports

Very Committed_____Not Committed

Television

Very Committed_____Not Committed

Friends

Very Committed_____Not Committed
                                    Church

Very Committed_____Not Committed
                                    Hobbies

Very Committed_____Not Committed
                                    Family

- **Reflect on your commitment to Jesus. What changes do you need to make as you seek to be fully committed to Him?**

Ask God to help you know what you need to change to surrender more fully to Him.

Read "Cody's Story."

Cody's Story

Cody is a young man who answered God's invitation. Following college, Cody moved to the country of Thailand in Southeast Asia to work with college students. One night, a student named Annan invited Cody to go to a movie. Before the movie began, a video was shown about the king of Thailand. Immediately, everyone in the theater stood up and applauded, including Annan. Some people even cried because they were so happy. When the movie ended Cody asked, "Why did everyone react with such emotion when the video about the king played?"

Annan said, "We love, respect, and honor our king. He is a king who cares for his people. Our king will often leave his palace and come to the villages and communities in Thailand to be with the people. The king wants to know and identify with the people. We know our king loves us, and we love him."

Cody knew Annan's description of the king of Thailand was preparing an opportunity for Cody to tell Annan about Jesus. In the days to come, Cody told Annan that God, the King over all the universe, loved us so much that He came to us in the person of Jesus. He came to identify with us, even to the point of taking all of our sin upon Himself, in order to save us and to make it possible for us to follow Him. Annan understood what Cody said. Annan became a follower of Jesus.

- **Why were the people so committed to the king of Thailand?**

- **How committed was the king to the people?**

- **How do you think Annan's commitment to the king helped Annan understand his commitment to God?**

WHY JESUS CAME

Read John 10:10.

- ● **Why did Jesus say He came to earth?**

- ● **What does it mean to "have life"?**

Jesus came to live the life we could not live and to die the death we all deserve. He came to earth to endure the punishment that we deserve—He took the punishment for US!

Throughout the Bible we can read about the impact of sin on people's relationships with God. Romans 3:23 tells us that everyone has sinned. Romans 6:23 says the payment for our sins is death.

When Jesus died on the cross He did not just take the punishment for our sins, He died in our place, as our substitute. Let me ask you another question. How can God have both a hatred for sin and a love for people at the same time? Let me explain the answer to this question.

When you read a book, you most likely look for the climax of the action. The climax is the turning point in the story. At this point, everything in the first part of the book makes sense and the following events resolve the storyline. The climax in the Bible is the cross. All the events recorded in the Bible before Jesus' death on the cross help us understand the sinfulness of man. This is the part of God's hatred of sin. At the cross, God showed both punishment and love. At the cross, God demonstrated how much He loves people. He loves us so much He allowed His one and only Son to die for us.

Does God hate sin?

Absolutely—look at the cross. Jesus took the punishment we deserve.

Does God love sinners?

Absolutely—look at the cross. Jesus saved us from all we deserve.

Jesus came to earth to do something no one else could ever do—He came to save us. We are saved from our sin not because of something we decided to do, but because God decided to do something. The love of God demonstrated in the life and death of Jesus is the ONLY foundation for salvation.

Have you ever heard someone say, "She is such a nice person, she is always doing things to help other people" or "She is such a great helper"? Many times we judge a person's character by the way she treats others. Do you ever judge someone's relationship to Jesus? How would people judge your relationship to Jesus based on your actions in these areas?

Low_____High

Prayer

Low_____High

Church attendance

Low_____High

Helping people

Low_____High

Being kind to others

Low_____High

Obeying the Ten Commandments

Low_____High

Obeying your parents

On the first day of this study you read John 3:1-21. Reread these verses.

Notice Jesus' words in verses 3 and 5. Jesus told Nicodemus that God would give people a new heart (not the one beating in your chest, a *new heart* means God would change their lives) and cleanse them of sin.

- **What type of changes does God need to make in your life?**

- **Are you willing for Him to make these changes? Why or why not?**

The Bible is very clear—there is nothing we can do to change our lives so that we always live in ways to please God. No matter how hard we work, how much we pray, how much we give, or how we love other people, sin still impacts our lives. The only way we become "clean" is through Jesus. Jesus is the only way to salvation. We must have faith in God to do what He says He will do through the death, burial, and resurrection of Jesus. Faith is knowing God will be pleased with us not because of anything we have done, but because of Jesus.

Once we receive the gift of forgiveness, that is not the end! That is just the beginning. God wants to work in our lives to change us. When we follow Jesus, we not only receive forgiveness, we receive the Holy Spirit. This is the central message of Jesus' calling—when a person becomes a Christian, he dies to himself and Jesus becomes his life. Jesus died so that He might live in each of us.

Think of it this way: When you come to Jesus …

His Spirit fills your spirit.

His love becomes your love.

His joy becomes your joy.

His mind becomes your mind.

His desires become your desires.

His will becomes your will.

His purpose becomes your purpose.

His power becomes your power.

The Christian life becomes nothing less than Jesus living in you.

Jesus has a purpose for your life. He is inviting you to join Him in fulfilling that purpose. Notice Jesus' words to Simon Peter, Andrew, James, and John, "Follow Me, and I will make you fishers of men." Jesus did not tell the men what He wanted them to do, He told them what He would CAUSE them to do. As Simon Peter, Andrew, James, and John followed Jesus, He changed everything about their lives: their thoughts, desires, wills, relationships, and purpose for which they lived.

What is Jesus causing you to do? In what ways is He changing your life so you can be His disciple? Is there anything in your life you are not willing to give up to follow Jesus? If so, tell God about it. Ask Him to help you let go so you can fully follow Jesus.

A WORD OF WARNING

During the time Jesus spent with the disciples He changed their lives. He equipped them so they could lead other people to follow Him. However, being fully-committed followers of Jesus cost the disciples. Read what is believed to have happened to some of Jesus' disciples.

- Peter preached to thousands of people about the life-changing power of Jesus. When Peter would not stop preaching, he was crucified upside down on a cross.
- Andrew was crucified in Greece.
- Judas (not Iscariot) was beaten to death.
- Thomas had a spear thrust into his side.
- James was beheaded.
- Philip was stoned to death.
- Matthew was burned at the stake.

Each of these men died for following Jesus. How committed do you think these men were to following Jesus? Do you have the same type of commitment? Why? What is different about what Jesus asked Simon Peter, Andrew, James, John, and the other disciples to do, than what Jesus asks us to do? In one word—NOTHING.

What is keeping you from being a fully-committed follower of Jesus?

God's Plan

God created EVERYTHING—including you and me. Since He created everything, God is in charge of everything. He rules over the whole earth. We belong to God. He created us to bring glory to Him. Sounds great, right? But something went wrong with God's plan. His plan was perfect, but man messed it up.

Adam and Eve, the first people, chose to disobey God. Since then, every person who has ever lived has chosen to disobey God (Romans 3:23). The Bible says disobeying God is sin. We do what we want to do instead of what God wants us to do. As a result of our sin, we are separated from God (Romans 6:23). We all deserve to be punished for our sins, but because God loves us and created us to bring glory to Him, He has a plan to save us.

- **What are some ways you have disobeyed God?**

God provided the only way to save us from our sin—Jesus.

Who is Jesus? He is God's one and only Son who came to earth and lived a perfect, sinless life (John 3:16). Jesus did not deserve any punishment, but because He loves us, He took the punishment we deserve for our sins.

- **How does it make you feel to know God loves you this much?**

Jesus paid the ultimate sacrifice for our sins, and we can know our sins are forgiven; however, this does not give us permission to sin and think "God will forgive me." We should try to live in ways that please and honor God—without sin. Since we are humans, we will continue to sin. When we ask God to forgive us, He will, but He allows us to face the consequences of our sins here on earth. For example, if you disobey your parents, you can ask God to forgive you and He will, however, you still face the consequences of disobeying your parents and may be grounded. If someone kills another person, he can ask God to forgive him, but he still faces the consequences of his actions—most likely jail or worse.

- **What are some consequences you face because of your sins?**

Jesus died on the cross in our place. Everything we have ever done wrong was paid for through Jesus dying on the cross. Because of His actions, we can be forgiven of all our sins! Through His death, burial, and resurrection we are provided forgiveness of our sins (Romans 5:8; 2 Corinthians 5:21; 1 Peter 3:18a).

- **Have you ever been punished for something you did not do? How did you feel?**

- **How do you feel knowing Jesus took the punishment for your sins?**

Jesus did not stay dead! God brought Him back to life. Many people saw Him after His resurrection, proving that He is alive! Soon, Jesus returned to heaven to be with God and rule over the world forever. He still rules today.

Why is it important that Jesus rose from the dead? When God brought Jesus back to life, God showed that He accepted the sacrifice Jesus provided. Jesus' actions took the punishment of our sins once and for all.

One day, Jesus will return to earth as King. When He does, the people who have not put their faith in God will be separated from God forever. The people who have put their faith in God will spend eternity in heaven with God (Acts 1:11; John 3:36).

HOW DOES A PERSON RESPOND TO JESUS?

Gospel means *GOOD NEWS!* God sent Jesus to live a perfect life. He did! Jesus willingly died on the cross in our place. Because of His actions, we can be a part of God's family.

Our response includes knowing who God is (a holy God) and who we are (sinners). We tell God we messed up (sinned) and that we are sorry for going our own way, doing our own thing, and turning away from Him (1 John 1:9).

We repent, and turn away from our sins. Repent does not mean just turning from doing bad things to doing good things. *Repent* means turning from our sins and turning to Jesus, trusting Him to save us.

To repent we must believe only Jesus can save us and we cannot save ourselves. Nothing we do—reading the Bible, praying, going to church, being kind, saying good things, or trying to live a perfect life—can save us. Our faith and trust in Jesus and what He did for us is the only thing that will save us (Ephesians 2:8-9).

Tell God and tell others what you believe—you are trusting in Jesus as your Savior and Lord. You can start following Him and living in His ways. You have a new life and look forward to being with God forever (Romans 10:9-10,13)!

If you are ready to trust Jesus as your Savior and Lord and receive His free gift of eternal life, call out to God and ask Him to save you. Admit to God you have disobeyed Him and your sin separates you from Him. Tell God you are sorry, and you deserve His punishment. Believe Jesus died on the cross in your place to take your punishment so your sins can be forgiven. Believe God raised Jesus from the dead so you might have victory over sin and death. Confess to God that, although you have been disobedient, you are counting on Jesus' life of perfect obedience and righteousness to make you acceptable before God. Ask God to enable you by His Holy Spirit to die to yourself and to follow Jesus as your Savior and Lord.

TRANSFORMING

- **When you hear the word *transformation*, what comes to mind?**

Seed to plant

Tadpole to frog

Baby to adult

- **How were these items transformed from what they began as into what they became?**

What causes transformation? Does a seed have a choice to transform into a plant? Does a tadpole have a choice to transform into a frog? Does a baby have a choice to transform into an adult? Why or why not? For most things, transformation naturally takes place over time. To serve its purpose, a seed must change, a tadpole must become a frog, and a baby must grow and develop. To serve our purpose as followers of Jesus, we must change.

How do you feel about transforming into a follower of Jesus? Just as with other things, this is usually not a sudden transformation. While our transformation began when we became Christians, transformation into a follower of Jesus is a lifelong process. This week we

transformation
to change completely

will discover some areas in our lives Jesus wants to transform, but before we talk about Jesus transforming us, let's understand something about Jesus.

We usually like to change things so they make us happy. If I don't like the color of my bedroom—I paint it. If I don't like the food at one restaurant—I eat somewhere else. If I don't like a certain television show—I change the channel. We grow up thinking if we don't like something—CHANGE IT. However, this does not work the same way with Jesus. We cannot change Jesus into what we want Him to be. In order to follow Jesus, we must let Him change us. Are you ready to get started with your transformation?

One of the reasons Jesus was such a great teacher is that He used objects and illustrations His followers could relate to. As Jesus and the disciples walked through a field or city, He pointed out things right in front of the disciples that helped them understand what He was teaching.

Read these verses. Match the verses with the items.

Matthew 6:28-30   **Mark 4:21-23**   **Luke 13:18-21**

- **What other items did Jesus use to teach His followers?**

Draw a plant with vines, branches, and fruit growing out of the flower pot.

Read John 15:5. Label the vine you drew *Jesus*. Write your name on one of the branches. (We will talk about the fruit on Day 5.)

►THINK ABOUT THIS

- **In John 15, Jesus used a vine to teach people about staying connected. In the illustration, to whom are the branches connected?**

- **What happens when a branch is no longer connected to a vine?**

A branch that is no longer connected to a vine will die because it cannot receive the needed nutrients. In addition, the branch cannot produce fruit. This branch cannot serve its purpose.

Jesus taught we are to stay connected to Him. When we are no longer connected to Jesus, we stop growing in Him, we lose the power He wants us to have, and we stop telling people about Him. As a result, we are not being the type of follower Jesus wants.

To be a follower of Jesus is to have a close relationship with Him. Remember—He is the Vine, we are the branches. In fact, Jesus lives in us and we live in Him! He is the source (cause) of transformation in our lives.

How does it make you feel to know Jesus lives in you?

Are there areas in your life you wish Jesus did not know about?

What would you like to change about these areas?

Do you feel connected to Jesus? In what ways?

Do you spend time each day praying?

Do you read your Bible every day?

Being a follower of Jesus means staying connected to the Vine. When you stay connected, you are transformed—changed in your actions, thoughts, attitudes, and desires. Jesus is changing you!

Ask God to show you areas of your life that need to be transformed. Ask Him to help you allow Him to transform you.

What are some of the biggest changes that have happened to you lately? Did you start a new school? Did you make new friends? In what ways has your body changed? Change cannot be stopped—EVERYTHING changes. Change is a part of life. Being a follower of Jesus means He will change you.

Let's think about the image of the vine we read about yesterday. Look back at your drawing (page 26). Which part of the drawing is Jesus? Which part are you? Let's discover more about the verses we read yesterday.

►SEARCH THE SCRIPTURES

Read John 15:1-5. In the boxes, draw pictures representing the branches.

Connected Branch	Disconnected Branch

- **Look at the branches. Which branch would you like to be? Why?**

- **Why is it important for branches to stay connected to the vine?**

►THINK ABOUT THIS

Disconnected branches cannot receive nutrients, so the branches die. They will no longer produce or grow fruit. Connected branches are growing, healthy, and ready to produce fruit.

You are probably wondering—*What does this have to do with me?* Once again, look back at the vine you drew yesterday. Remember, you are the branch and Jesus is the Vine. If you do not stay connected to Him, you stop growing and do not fulfill the purpose He designed for you.

The next question you are probably wondering is, *How do I stay connected to Jesus?* Check out a few ways you can stay connected to Jesus:

1. **Read and study your Bible.** Learn as much as you can about Jesus. As long as you live, continue learning.

2. **Pray.** Tell God what you think and how you feel. Listen to Him. He will speak to and help you.

3. **Worship God.** Spending time in worship helps you have the strength you need to continue following Jesus.

4. **Tell people what you believe.** The more you tell people about Jesus, the easier it becomes.

5. **Ask someone to keep you accountable.** That means someone helps you know when you do not live in ways that please and honor God. Your friend must be honest with you about the way you act, what you say, or other things you do that need to be corrected.

Just remember—the more connected we are to Jesus, the better we will grow and transform into the follower He desires.

Changes are not easy. However, if we are to become the followers of Jesus He wants us to become, we must be willing to change. Tomorrow we will begin to look at some areas Jesus wants to change in our lives. Before we get there, let's see what changes you think need to be made. List five things you think Jesus needs to change about you. Be honest. You will not be asked to show your list to anyone.

1.

2.

3.

4.

5.

Now that you have your list, tell God about these things. Tell Him why you feel you need to change in these areas. Let me give you a word of warning: Do not ask God to do something you are not committed to changing. When God starts working in your life, changes are going to take place!

Have you ever thought about how powerful your mind is? Read these facts about your brain.

- **The left side of your brain is better at problem solving, math, and writing.**

- **The right side of your brain is the more creative side. This side is good at art and music.**

- **Your brain stores a lot of information in the memory, including facts, figures, and all the smells, tastes, and things you have seen, heard, or touched.**

- **Your brain receives and processes information faster than a supercomputer.**

- **The structure of your brain changes each time you learn something.**

Our brains are a very powerful part of our bodies. They are also one of the areas Jesus wants to change. Read these verses related to the brain. What do these verses tell you about your mind?

Matthew 22:37　　　　　　　**Romans 8:5-7**　　　　　　　**Colossians 3:2**

Jesus wants to change our minds so we think more like Him. If your parents, teachers, and friends could see everything you think, how would you feel? Would it embarrass you for people to know what you think? How would you feel if Jesus knew everything you were thinking? Ready for this? He already knows what you are thinking. You cannot hide your thoughts from Him.

SEARCH THE SCRIPTURES

Read Romans 12:1-2.

- **What do you think Paul meant when he wrote these words?**

- **How can God transform your mind?**

- **How does the world impact your thoughts?**

When our minds change, we stop following the sinful ways of the world and we follow Jesus. When Jesus transforms our minds, He changes what we believe, our attitudes, and our actions. What would your life be like if Jesus controlled your thoughts?

Before we talk about another area of change, answer these questions:

- **If you could be any person in the world, who would you be?**

- **If you could live anywhere in the world, where would you live?**

- **If you could own anything in the world, what would you own?**

- **If you could do anything in the world, what would you do?**

- **Why did you choose the things you wrote down?**

- **Read the definition of** *desire*. **What are some other things you desire? How do your desires impact the way you live?**

How would you feel if Jesus asked you to give away everything you owned? Would you do it? Why or why not? Would you be willing to leave your friends to follow Jesus? Why or why not?

desire

to long for; want

Many people are not willing to give up things that keep them from being fully-committed followers of Jesus. They do not trust Jesus to provide what they need.

Think about the disciples. Read Matthew 4:18-22.

- **How did Simon Peter, Andrew, James, and John respond when Jesus called them?**

Did Jesus tell the men to go home and pack a suitcase, then come follow Him? No! While we do not know what the men took with them as they traveled with Jesus, we can know they did not take much, if anything. The men walked everywhere they traveled, so taking things with them would become a problem. The men left their families and friends, and gave up their jobs to follow Jesus.

Becoming a follower of Jesus is costly. We must be willing to give up everything we own to follow Jesus. Does that mean Jesus wants you to get rid of everything, drop out of school, or leave your family and friends to follow Him? Most likely not, but He wants you to be *willing* to give up everything. He does not want anything or anyone to become more important to you than He is.

- **Is there anything in your life that you are not willing to give up to follow Jesus? Why?**

- **Think about everything you own and the people in your life. Are any of these items or people keeping you from following Jesus?**

Thank God for everything He has given you. Ask Him to help you be willing to give up everything to follow Him.

Think about the ways you treat people. Circle the words that describe your actions.

Kind	**Helpful**	**Degrading**
Mean	**Supportive**	**Disrespectful**
Loving	**Abusive**	

Now draw a box around the words that show how Jesus treated people.

Compare your life to Jesus' life.

- **In what ways are you the same?**

- **How are you different?**

When we begin to think like Jesus and want the same things He wants, it is only a matter of time before we start acting like Him. We live according to His will instead of our own. How does it make you feel to know you can live like Jesus? Does that mean you will move to Jerusalem, walk everywhere you go, and eat the foods Jesus ate? No. Jesus wants you to act like Him where you are TODAY.

Let's read about a time Jesus did not follow cultural rules.

SEARCH THE SCRIPTURES

Read John 4:1-26. Check the actions Jesus demonstrated.

___ Spoke to the woman.

___ Told the woman about God.

___ Ignored the woman because she was a Samaritan.

___ Respected the woman.

___ Told the woman about her past.

___ Made fun of the woman because of the sins in her life.

___ Asked the woman to have her husband bring Him a drink of water.

Look back at Jesus' actions. Let's examine the setting of these events and what makes Jesus' actions so amazing.

- During this time, the Jewish people did not like the Samaritans (the Samaritans did not like the Jews either). In fact, when Jews traveled through the area, they would go out of their way to avoid the area of Sychar (SIGH kahr), where the Samaritans lived. Women typically came to the well early in the morning when it was cooler. This woman was not accepted by the other women and came to the well by herself around noon. (Notice her living condition—she'd had five husbands and was not married to the man she currently lived with.) Most likely the other women of the city did not want anything to do with her.

- For a Jewish man (Jesus) to speak to a Samaritan woman was against the customs.

With this information in mind, reread John 4:1-26.

- **How did Jesus break tradition? What was the result of Jesus' actions?**

- **Think about your life. Are there people you do not speak to? How do you treat people at school, on the school bus, in your neighborhood, in your family?**

- **In what ways does Jesus need to change your life for you to treat people like He would treat them?**

OK, you are probably thinking, *Jesus did this because He is God's Son.* Let's look at how Jesus helped Simon Peter learn he should not show favoritism. Acts 10 tells us about a man named Cornelius (kawr NEE lih uhs), a member of the Italian army. Cornelius was a Gentile (a non-Jew) who worshiped God. One day, God told Cornelius to send some of his men for Peter. In a dream, God showed Peter not to show favoritism to anyone. When the men arrived where Peter was staying, they told him why they had come. Peter invited the men into the home. The next day they traveled back to Cornelius' home. Peter helped Cornelius learn about God. What does Acts 10:34 say God taught Peter?

- **Are there times you do not treat people with respect?**

favoritism
the favoring of one person or group over others with equal claims; partiality

- **Is God pleased with how you treat everyone?**

- **What does God need to change in your life for you to become a follower of Jesus?**

Are you willing to make the changes? If so, tell God. Read John 15:12-15. Write a prayer using these verses as a guide.

Pray for your family, friends, schoolmates, neighbors, and even the strangers you meet. Ask God to help you live in ways that tell people they are important and that God loves them. Ask God to forgive you of times you treated people in inappropriate ways or said things about people you should not have said.

Can you believe you are already a preteen? In just a few years you will be driving, graduating high school, and going to college. Have you thought about what job you would like to have when you grow up? Why do you want that job? How would you feel if God asked you to become something else?

Being a follower of Jesus means you do what Jesus wants you to do instead of what you want to do. When you begin to follow Jesus, you have a new purpose in this world. As followers of Jesus, we live to fulfill what Jesus wants. So, what is our purpose?

▶ SEARCH THE SCRIPTURES

Read John 15:5.

purpose
the reason for which something exists or is done, made, or used

- **What does John 15:5 say is your purpose?**

- **What does it mean to "bear fruit"?**

▶ THINK ABOUT THIS

Read "The Wrong Beliefs."

The Wrong Beliefs

Many Muslims believe that Jesus did not die on a cross nor was He raised from the dead. They teach that the man who died on the cross was a man who looked like Jesus. (This belief was started by the prophet Mohammed 600 years after Jesus' crucifixion.)

Other people believe Jesus was actually on the cross, but that He did not die. He was simply hurt really, really, really bad. He fainted and became unconscious, making people think He was dead. After being wrapped in grave clothes and put in a tomb He became conscious, moved the stone out of the way, snuck passed the guards, and walked away.

Another group of people believe Mary and Mary Magdalene went to the wrong tomb and mistakenly thought Jesus had risen.

Another belief about Jesus' death blames the disciples. Some people believe the disciples stole Jesus' body. Some say the disciples were crazy and made up the story of Jesus' resurrection.

- **What do these statements tell you about people's beliefs about Jesus?**

Think about the people who helped you learn about Jesus. Compare their actions to Jesus' actions.

Jesus spent time with His disciples teaching and helping them know about God. Just before He returned to heaven, Jesus told the disciples to go throughout the whole world teaching people about Him.

- **Are you willing to tell people about Jesus? Why or why not?**

- **Does it scare you to think about God sending you to go to another country to tell people about Jesus?**

- **Are you willing to tell people about Jesus in your neighborhood or school?**

Being a follower of Jesus means we have a purpose, and that purpose is to bear fruit.

Read "A Visit to India."

A Visit to India

If you have never been to India, just think PEOPLE. Lots and lots and lots of people. Approximately 1.2 billion people live in India—over 600 million of them live in the northern part where I was visiting. The streets are very crowded. Many villages span the countryside. Because the economy is so bad, many of the people live in poverty (in fact, more people in India live in poverty than the whole population of the United States). India is not just in poverty in economic ways, the country is also in poverty spiritually. Only about 0.5% of the people are Christians, meaning 99.5% of the people do not believe in Jesus.

As I looked around me one day, I thought to myself, Who am I to come to India to tell people what they need to believe? Who am I to tell them the gods they worship are false, and that Jesus is the only true God? And who am I to tell the people that if they do not turn from their sin and trust in Jesus, they will spend eternity in hell?

At the end of the day, we don't tell people that their own beliefs are wrong because we are smarter or richer or because we think we are better than them. We share the good news of Jesus because God is in charge, and He has told us to tell people about the only way to be saved—by turning from our sin and trusting Jesus as Savior and Lord. We don't point to our own goodness; we point to God's grace.

My visit to India helped me see the importance of telling people about God and how they could have a relationship with Him through His Son Jesus. You may never get to visit India, but did you know there are people all around you who need to hear about Jesus?

Look back at the picture you drew of the vine, branches, and fruit on Day 1 (page 26). Think about five people you know who are not Christians. Write their initials on the fruit. Pray for opportunities to "bear fruit" with these people.

How do you feel about the things we talked about this week? Are you challenged? Are you ready for the task? Are you committed to following Jesus?

I want to take a minute and point out a few words you may have skipped over in John 15:5. Reread this verse. Now read it out loud. What must take place for us to produce fruit?

In what ways does a person *abide* in Jesus? How does He *abide* in His followers? Read the definition of *abide*.

- **How does it make you feel to know Jesus abides in you?**

▶ **SEARCH THE SCRIPTURES**

abide
to remain; continue; stay

Read John 15:5-10.

- **How many times do these verses tell you to abide in Jesus?**

- **What are the benefits of abiding in Him?**

I can promise you, abiding in Jesus is NOT easy. You will be tempted to do things, say things, and act in ways that are not pleasing and honoring to God. (Even Simon Peter denied knowing Jesus when Peter thought his life was in danger.) Jesus promised He will never leave us. When He returned to heaven, God sent the Holy Spirit to live in His followers. The Holy Spirit helps us learn about God, and gives us the strength to live in ways that please and honor God. The Holy Spirit also empowers people to tell about Jesus.

▶ **THINK ABOUT THIS**

Read "A Trip to East Asia."

A Trip to East Asia

A few years ago, my wife Heather and I traveled to a part of East Asia where very few people have ever heard of Jesus. While we were there, Heather repeatedly shared the gospel with a girl named Meilin. Meilin seemed to listen as Heather told her about Jesus, yet she resisted Jesus as Lord. Heather and I asked God to give us the words, wisdom, and grace we needed to help Meilin know how much He loved her.

After a couple of weeks, it was time for us to leave Meilin's town. We packed our bags and said goodbye to the people. While we waited for our ride we could hear the Christians talking, praying, and studying the Bible.

> *Meilin rushed up to Heather and began to tell her how she was turning from her sin and trusting in Jesus. As Meilin shared with Heather, the group inside the house was reading aloud Psalm 46:10. I looked over and saw tears streaming down Heather's face as she prayed with Meilin. I heard the group inside the house saying these words, "Be still and know that I am God. I will be exalted among the nations, I will be exalted in the earth." Immediately, I was reminded that the Savior who reigns at the right hand of the Father is ready to give His disciples everything they need to exalt His name all over the world.*

How did Heather have the power to tell Meilin about Jesus? What do you think would have happened if Heather had decided not to abide in Jesus? As followers of Jesus, we will face difficult situations. The Bible tells us Jesus is seated at the right hand of God, but that is not all Jesus is doing. He is interceding (praying) for us every day. He is committed to giving us everything we need to tell every person on the planet about Himself.

Are you up for the challenge?

Write the words of John 3:16 here.

- **Do you believe God loved the world so much that He sent Jesus? __ Yes __ No**

Read John 3:18.

- **Do you believe that anyone who does not believe in Jesus as Savior and Lord is already judged (condemned)? __ Yes __ No**

Read John 14:6. What does this verse tell us about Jesus?

Jesus is the _____.

Jesus is the _____.

Jesus is the _____.

- **Do you believe these things about Jesus? ___ Yes ___ No**

If you believe these things, then pray and ask God to help you follow Jesus as Lord, abide in Him, and make disciples.

Reread "Caleb's Story" (page 19).

After Heather, Caleb, and I returned from Kazakhstan, we quickly learned that people can ask some of the strangest questions. Here are two of the questions people asked us the most.

"He's so cute. Do you have children of your own?"

"Have you met his real mother?"

How do you think I responded? To the first question, I would say, "Come in real close so you can hear the secret I want to share. Caleb is ours!" In answering the second question, I would say, "Well, yes, I'm actually married to her. Her name is Heather." Then people would say, "You know what I mean," to which I would respond, "Yes, and you know what I mean. My precious wife is not his fake mother, she's real."

Read the definition of *adopt*.

adopt
to take as one's own

- **What comes to mind when you hear the word *adopt*?**

- **Do you know anyone who was adopted? How has being adopted changed the person's life?**

Our son, Caleb belongs to my wife and me—he is OURS. He is not a stranger in our family. He is not somewhat our son, partly our son, or kind-of our son. He is FULLY, 100% our son (for the good and the bad). When Heather and I returned home with Caleb, that was not the end of his story. Instead, it was just the beginning of a great adventure. Caleb knows I am his dad and he's my son, not just because I loved him enough to go to Kazakhstan to adopt him, but because of the love I show him every day. His being a part of our family is not only based on an adoption paper signed by a judge, but is based on the relationship we have every day as we play cars, throw a baseball, chase each other around the yard, and sing together.

As I listen to people talk about our adoption, I wonder if we truly understand what it means to be adopted by God—to be a part of His family. Let's explore what it means to be adopted by God into His family.

Think about how many times a day you hear or say the word *love*. Complete these statements.

I love eating _____ .

I love watching _____ .

I love it when you _____ .

I love having you _____ .

I love _____ .

We could go on listing things we "love." If we are not careful, we put the same emphasis on loving things as we do on loving people, and ultimately on loving God. We may say "we love God" with the same meaning as "we love eating Mexican food."

Read the definition of *love*.

love
great and warm affection

Heather and I love Caleb. If we did not love him, we would not have adopted him into our family. Have you ever thought about how much God loves you? He loves you so much He sent Jesus to earth. Only through Jesus' life, death, and resurrection can we be adopted into God's family. Only by being adopted into God's family can we call Him "Father."

In the Old Testament, God is rarely described as "Father." In fact, the reference to God as "Father" only occurs 15 times in the Old Testament. In the New Testament, God is described as "Father" 165 times—164 of these descriptions take place as Jesus taught His disciples.

- **Why do you think the New Testament refers to God more as "Father" than the Old Testament?**

- **How does it make you feel to know you can call God "Father"?**

Throughout the Old Testament, God is called by many names. Read these Scripture passages about some of God's names.

Name	Reference	Meaning
Elohim	Genesis 1:1	Powerful God
Adonai	Malachi 1:6	LORD of Hosts
El Elyon	Genesis 14:17-20	The Most High God
El Shaddai	Psalm 91:1	God Almighty
Yahweh	Exodus 3:14	I AM
Jehovah Jireh	Genesis 22:13-14	The LORD Will Provide
Jehovah Rophe	Exodus 15:26	The LORD Our Healer
Jehovah Nissi	Exodus 17:15	The LORD Is Our Banner
Jehovah Mekadesh	Exodus 31:13	The LORD Who Sanctifies You
Jehovah Shalom	Judges 6:24	The LORD Is Peace
Jehovah Tsidkenu	Jeremiah 23:6	The LORD Is Our Righteousness
Jehovah Shammah	Ezekiel 48:35	The LORD Who Is Present

SEARCH THE SCRIPTURES

Read Matthew 6:9-13.

- **What feelings do you experience as you read these verses?**

- **How do Jesus' words help you relate to God as "Father"?**

Read the following verses. What do they tell you about God, the Father?

Matthew 6:9-15

Matthew 6:25-33

1 Corinthians 8:6

2 Corinthians 1:3

Hebrews 12:5-11

Read 1 John 3:1.

- **How does it make you feel to know God loves you and wants to adopt you into His family?**

As a follower of Jesus, you have been adopted into God's family. Everyone who is a follower of Jesus also has God as his Father. He wants you to love Him.

- **How do you know God loves you?**

- **How do you tell God you love Him?**

- **When did you last take time to thank God for adopting you into His family?**

As we end today's study, let me tell you about an experience I had with Caleb. Read "I Love You, Daddy."

I Love You, Daddy

For a time, Caleb and I were doing this thing where I would point at him across the room and yell, "I love Caleb!" Then he would look back at me and yell, "I love Daddy."

One day we were doing this and Caleb was laughing until all of the sudden he stopped, looked at me, and said, "You love me?"

I said, "Yeah, buddy, I do."

And then he asked what seems to be his favorite question: "Why?"

I said, "Because you're my son."

So he asked the question again, "Why?"

This time I thought to myself: Now that's a good question. Out of all the children in the world, why is this precious little boy standing in front of me my son? I thought about all of the things that had come together for Heather and me to adopt Caleb. Eventually I said to Caleb, "You are our son because we wanted you. And we came to get you so that you might have a mommy and a daddy."

If you don't remember anything else from today's study, remember this—God loves us and wants us to be a part of His family. He gave up more than we can imagine so that we might have the privilege of being His children. As a follower of Jesus, don't accept His love lightly. Take time to enjoy being in His family.

Thank God for adopting you into His family.

Make a list of 10 things you need.

1.

2.

3.

4.

5.

6.

7.

8.

9.

10.

Read the definitions of *need* and *want*, then circle the things in your list that are wants instead of needs.

Desires (to long for; want) are normal for everyone. We all have things we want. Just look at your list and see how much you want. Do you want the same things as your best friend? Probably not! Each of us has our own wants; that is one of the ways God created us unique. Imagine how the world would be if we all wanted the same thing—the same flavor of ice cream, the same style of shoes, the same color of bicycle, or to live in the same house. Aren't you glad God made us unique?

need
something necessary or useful

want
a wish for something; desires

Yesterday we talked about being adopted into God's family. When a person is adopted into a family, she becomes a part of everything the family owns and does. Within the family, the child soon develops her wants. This is normal. We focus on OUR wants and needs. Can you think of a word that describes this? The word is *selfish*. We put our wants and needs before those of others.

As a part of God's family, we need to focus on what He wants. We should live the way—He wants. We should treat people the way—He wants. We should _____ (you fill in the blank) the way—He wants. I know, you're thinking, *How do I do that?* Let me see if I can help you understand.

Let's go all the way back to the garden of Eden. Picture the garden in your mind. What types of plants and animals do you see? What type of food is provided? Draw a picture of the way you imagine the garden of Eden.

SEARCH THE SCRIPTURES

Read Genesis 2:8-9.

- **What do these verses say about what God provided Adam and Eve?**

Notice verse 9 says that trees were pleasant to look at as well as good for food.

- **What are some things you see that are pleasing to look at?**

- **What are things you desire to eat?**

In the garden of Eden, Adam and Eve had needs and desires—and all of the needs and desires were met by God.

- **Do you trust God to provide for your needs and desires? How?**

Read Genesis 3:1-7.

- **What did Adam and Eve give in to?**

- **How did their actions change their relationship with God?**

Adam and Eve gave in to their desires. As a result, their relationship with God was forever changed. Adam and Eve believed Satan's lie that their desires could only be fulfilled apart from God. In order to have what they wanted, Adam and Eve disobeyed God.

Have you ever made the same mistake as Adam and Eve? OK, you have probably not eaten fruit from a forbidden tree, but what about your desires and wants? Do you ever do, say, think, or act in ways that are opposite to what God says to do? We all have! That is what the Bible calls SIN. When Adam and Eve disobeyed God, sin entered the world. According to Romans 3:23, who has sinned?

The answer to that question is EVERYONE! All 7 billion of us currently living on earth, everyone who has ever lived on earth, and everyone who will ever live on earth! Everyone except for Jesus!

THINK ABOUT THIS

Throughout His ministry, Jesus met the needs of people. He healed the sick, fed people when they were hungry, and helped people get what they needed. However, He did not just meet physical needs. He helped people get what they needed spiritually. In John 6 we read about Jesus feeding 5,000+ people with only five loaves of bread and two fish. The next day, the people came back to Jesus because they were hungry again. Jesus told the people that the food He provided for them only met their physical needs (they were no longer hungry), but He challenged the people to believe in God to have their spiritual needs met. Jesus recalled how God provided manna for the Israelites to eat while they were in the wilderness (Exodus 16). The people still did not understand what Jesus was saying because they focused on their physical needs. Read Jesus' words recorded in John 6:35. Jesus told the people that He was sent by God to satisfy their needs and desires.

Look back at your list of needs (page 45). If Jesus made a list of needs for you, what would He include? Would He include any of these items?

Need to pray more

Need to read and study your Bible more

Need to worship God more

Need to tell your friends about God and His Son Jesus

Need to ask someone to forgive you

Need to obey your parents

To be followers of Jesus, our needs and wants must be the same as His. How committed are you to allowing Jesus to change your needs and wants?

Pray that you will trust God to meet your needs as you become a follower of Jesus.

- How do you define *happiness*?

Circle the items that make you happy.

- What is it about these items that makes you happy?

- Do preteens desire to have the best cell phone, latest style of clothing, and be the most popular at school? Why?

- Does having these things bring long-lasting happiness?

SEARCH THE SCRIPTURES

Read John 10:10.

- What did Jesus say was His purpose in coming to earth?

- What does it mean to "have life"?

"Having life" does not mean Jesus will give you everything you want. Neither does it mean you will never face difficult or challenging days.

Read John 10:7-18.

- List the things Jesus says a shepherd does.

- How does it make you feel to know Jesus is your Shepherd and does these things for you?

- **How do Jesus' actions provide happiness for you?**

pleasures
a feeling of enjoyment; wish; something that pleases or delights

THINK ABOUT THIS

Look back at John 10:7-18. What actions do the sheep do? Do you see yourself as the sheep described in these verses? Here's the point—sometimes we are caught in the middle. We know we are supposed to follow Jesus, yet deep down the pleasures, pursuits, and possessions of the world appear far more exciting. So we choose to live the same way non-Christians live. We say we have faith in Jesus, yet we are just as influenced by the world as non-Christians.

pursuits
things followed after in order to catch or own

possessions
the act of holding as one's own; things that are held as one's own property

- **Do you agree or disagree with my last statement? Why?**

  ☐ **Agree**   ☐ **Disagree**

- **In what ways have you struggled between knowing what God wants you to do and doing what you want to do?**

- **How did you decide what to do?**

- **How did your decision impact your life?**

Let's look back at John 4:4-26, the story of Jesus and the woman at the well. (We read this story on Day 4 of Week 2.) Notice how Jesus called attention to the sins in the woman's life (v. 18). Why did Jesus call attention to her sins? I believe Jesus did this so she could see how messed up her life was. She was trying to find happiness in things outside of God's will. She had allowed things of the world to impact her life. Were these things making her happy? No, her life was a mess.

Jesus offered the woman a better way of living—follow Him. To be a follower of Jesus means we find our happiness in Him. We give up wanting "things" we think will bring us happiness to discover Jesus gives us everything we need. Let me summarize it this way: We must always remember that our deepest desires are not for *something*, but for *Someone*. Our ultimate happiness is found not in the things we enjoy, but in the Giver who provides them.

Make a list of all the things God has given you. (Write small; you should have a long list.) Now, one-by-one, thank God for these things. Ask God to help you focus on happiness in Jesus, not in the things you own.

Check off the chores you are responsible for doing in your family.

___ Feeding the dog	___ Mowing the yard	___ Dusting the furniture
___ Taking out the trash	___ Making your bed	___ Pulling weeds
___ Cooking dinner	___ Washing the clothes	___ Caring for siblings
___ Sweeping the floor	___ Bringing in the mail	___Cleaning the bathroom

How many times do your parents have to ask you to complete your chores before you actually do them?

I have met very few people who enjoy doing chores. Most of the time we approach these jobs without much motivation. We don't really want to do them, but we know they are necessary, so we rush to complete them.

I'm afraid many followers of Jesus have added a number of "religious chores" into their daily lives. They believe there are certain tasks every Christian must perform, even if they lack the motivation. Check out some actions that can become "religious chores."

___ **Read the Bible**	___ **Go to church**
___ **Pray**	___ **Tell people about Jesus**

Many Christians use these "religious chores" as ways to justify their actions. For example, some people may say watching an inappropriate television show is OK if they spend more time reading the Bible or praying. Others think the way they treat people does not matter as long as they go to church on Sunday morning.

READING THE BIBLE

To non-Christians, reading the Bible seems like a waste of time. How would you respond to someone who says, "You are wasting your time reading the Bible. The Bible is just a lot of stuff about things that happened a long time ago"?

To followers of Jesus, reading the Bible is an important part of our spiritual growth. We read the Bible to learn more about Jesus and how to live in ways that please and honor God. Christians aren't just to read the Bible, we are to think about what we read. We are to enjoy the Bible. We are to apply what the Bible says to every situation in our lives.

Read Psalm 19:7-11; 119:97-99; 119:169-176.

- **What do these verses say about reading and studying the Bible?**

Read Matthew 4:1-11. Following His time in the wilderness, Jesus was hungry. Satan tempted Jesus to turn stones into bread. How did Jesus respond? Jesus quoted Scripture. For followers of Jesus, reading the Bible is not a "religious chore," it is something we WANT to do. Reading the Bible helps Christians know how to stand up against the temptations in our lives.

So what about you? Do you love the Bible? When you read it, do you discover and apply things to your life? Do the words make a difference in your life?

PRAYING

Can you complete these prayers?

Now I lay me down to sleep ...

God is great, God is good ...

You may have said these prayers since you were a preschooler.

Another area that can become a "religious chore" is prayer. Followers of Jesus need to communicate with God. We need to feel connected to Jesus and involve Him in every decision we face. However, if we are not careful, we think of prayer as simply asking for things. We may say, "God help me, protect me, give me!" Our prayers end up being lists of things we need and stuff we want.

- **Do your prayers ever sound like "give me" lists? When?**

The purpose of prayer is not for Jesus' followers to tell God something. The purpose is to experience time WITH God. That's why Jesus said to His followers to get alone by yourself when you pray (Matthew 6:6).

- **Where is a place you can spend time praying to God?**

Let me challenge you to pray. I believe praying will completely change your life. Something happens that cannot be described in words when you get alone with God. In a quiet place, behind closed doors, when we talk with God, we experience a joy to which no person or no thing can ever begin to compare.

- **How happy are you with the amount of time you spend praying? Why?**

Very happy   **Happy**   **Unhappy**   **Very unhappy**

- **What do you need to change in your life to have a better prayer time?**

Tomorrow we will examine two more areas that can become "religious chores." For now, take time to think about how long you spend reading your Bible and praying. Find a quiet place and talk with God. Tell Him the struggles you face reading your Bible and praying. Ask God to help you develop an attitude of "get to" instead of "have to" about reading the Bible and praying in your quiet time, as well as throughout the rest of the day.

Yesterday we talked about two ways we grow as followers of Jesus. Do you remember these two ways?

- Read and study the _____ .

- _____ .

Have you completed your chores today? Did you make your bed, clean your room, put your dirty socks in the laundry basket? Did you do these things without your mom or dad having to remind you? If not, put your book down and go do them, then come back and finish today's activities.

Let's examine another area that can become a "religious chore" if we are not careful.

WORSHIPING

How would you respond to these questions?

- **What is *worship*?**

- **Whom do you worship?**

- **Why do you worship?**

- **When and where do you worship?**

For followers of Jesus, we worship God because we WANT to. We praise God because we enjoy Him. Read the definition of *worship*. As followers of Jesus, we gladly use our lips and our lives to praise the One we love above all others.

Read the definition of *delight*.

- **Do you "delight" in God?**

- **How does it make you feel that the Creator of EVERYTHING wants to have a relationship with YOU?**

worship
giving honor, reverence, and praise to God

delight
to take great pleasure

The Bible tells us that every part of life is to be an act of worship. Every experience is an opportunity to declare our delight in God and praise His name.

- **Apart from worshiping at church, when do you worship God?**

- **Do you think God is pleased with your worship of Him? Why or why not?**

- **What do you need to do to make every part of your life an act of worship?**

SEARCH THE SCRIPTURES

Read Acts 16:25-34.

- **Why had Paul and Silas been arrested?**

- **How did they respond to their situation?**

- **How did the other prisoners respond to Paul and Silas?**

THINK ABOUT THIS

Paul and Silas were in JAIL and yet they sang and praised God. What happened as a result of their commitment to God? Following an earthquake, all of the chains fell off of the prisoners. The guard who was responsible for the prisoners prepared to kill himself because he thought they had escaped, but none of the prisoners left the jail. As a result of their actions, Paul and Silas were able to tell the guard and his whole family about Jesus.

Place yourself in Paul and Silas' position. You are sitting in a jail cell.

- **Would you worship God? Why or why not?**

- **Where are some challenging places you find yourself?**

- **Do you worship God in these places?**

- **What do your actions say to people about your commitment to following Jesus?**

Take time to listen to several praise songs. How does music affect your worship?

If you wrote a praise song to God, what would you say? Take time to write some words of praise to God.

Now read or sing your praise song to God.

Let's explore two more areas that can help us grow as followers of Jesus. The first of these areas may be something you have not heard talked about much—fasting.

FASTING

- **When you hear the word *fast* what comes to mind?**

Did you think about a fast car, a fast plane, or completing your homework in record time? That is not the meaning of *fast* I want us to examine. Read the definition of *fast*.

The idea of fasting may be new to you, but Jesus implied the disciples should regularly set aside food in order to focus on God.

> ### SEARCH THE SCRIPTURES

Read Matthew 6:16-18.

fast
giving up something like food or drink for an extended period of time in order to pray, seek guidance, and find satisfaction in God alone

- **What guidelines did Jesus give the disciples when they fasted?**

> ### THINK ABOUT THIS

The Bible describes three forms of fasting. The first involves completely going without food. This is the type of fast Jesus followed while spending 40 days in the wilderness (Luke 4:2). During these 40 days, Jesus ate nothing. A second type of fasting lasted for three days. In Acts 9:9, we read about Paul fasting following his encounter with Jesus on the road to Damascus. During this time, Paul went without food or drink. This type of fast is also mentioned in Ezra 10:6 and Esther 4:16. The third type of fast is a *partial fast*. This is the type of fast Daniel followed, meaning he did not stop eating or drinking everything, only specific items, such as meat. (For you and me that may mean we stop eating desserts or hamburgers—or even pizza.) You may even want to fast from some activities you participate in, such as watching television, using the computer, playing video games, talking on the phone, texting, or playing sports.

You may be wondering, *What's the purpose of fasting?* When a person fasts, he is seeking to know God better (Isaiah 58). Fasting can be an effective way to reflect on any confessions you need to make as well as help you have a more meaningful prayer time (Ezra 8:23; Joel 2:12). When the early church wanted to know God's plan, there was a time of prayer and fasting (Acts 13).

Let me give you a word of warning about fasting. Fasting should be done as a private act of worship before God. When a person fasts, she should not say to everyone, "I'm fasting! Don't ask me if I want anything to eat" (Exodus 34:28; 1 Samuel 7:6; Matthew 6:17-18).

If you have never fasted before, talk with your parents and get their permission for you to do so. Let me encourage you to start by giving up one meal each week. Instead of eating breakfast, lunch, or dinner one day, use the hour to read your Bible and pray.

When you get used to doing this during one meal, plan to fast for two meals in one day, and then for an entire 24-hour period. (Again, make sure you talk with your parents and explain to them what you are doing.)

GIVING

Let's examine one more way we can grow as a part of God's family. When you think about growing in your love for God, giving may not be the first thing that comes to your mind. However, Jesus' teaching on giving was directly connected to His teaching on fasting and praying.

▶ SEARCH THE SCRIPTURES

Read Matthew 6:19-24.

- **What did Jesus say would happen to the treasures people collected on earth?**

Our hearts tend to reflect our priorities. Our hearts are not just the muscle in our chest that pumps blood throughout our bodies. In the Bible, the heart refers to making choices, believing in God, and allowing God to work through us.

- **Where did Jesus say your heart would be?**

- **What did Jesus mean when He said no one can serve two masters?**

▶ THINK ABOUT THIS

Notice what Jesus said about money and love. According to Jesus, our money (and other things we own) does not just reflect our hearts. Jesus was teaching His followers that if money was the most important part of their lives, then God could not be. How important is money in your life? What about the other things you own—are they more important to you than God? I want you to know that owning things is not wrong, but the problem comes when we put more emphasis on the things we own than on God.

One of the best ways to grow in our love for God is to give our resources in obedience to Him. One day, Jesus and some of the disciples were sitting in the temple. Jesus noticed the people giving their offerings. Many rich people were putting in a lot of money. A poor widow came and dropped in two tiny coins worth hardly anything. Jesus gathered the disciples close to Him and said, "This woman has given more than anyone in the temple. The other people gave out of their abundance, but this woman gave everything she has to live on" (Mark 12:41-44).

- **What did Jesus want the disciples to learn about giving?**

- **What had the disciples given up to follow Jesus?**

- **What can you learn from the widow's example?**

- **What are your current habits when it comes to giving your money? Your time? Your talents?**

Do you give because of a "religious chore" or out of your love to God?

This week we talked about ways we can grow in our relationship with Jesus. I don't want you to think these areas are the only ways we grow. We also grow as we tell people about Jesus, deal with challenges in our everyday lives, trust God when we don't know what to do, and completely surrender our lives to Him.

Go to your quiet place and spend time talking with God. Ask Him to show you any areas of your life you need to improve in relation to serving Him. Invite God to show you how you can better enjoy Him.

Have you ever wondered, *Why am I on this earth?* or *What is my purpose in life?* How did you respond?

Recall the words of Jesus when He invited Simon Peter and Andrew to follow Him (Matthew 4:19). What did Jesus say His followers would be?

- **When was the last time you were a "fisher of men"?**

Read Acts 1:8. Jesus said these words to His followers just before He returned to heaven.

- **According to this verse, when will a follower of Jesus receive power?**

- **As a result of receiving power, what will happen to the person?**

Let's put the four places Jesus mentioned into our present living places. Write the name of your city, state, and country on the blanks.

Jerusalem = _____ **(your city)**

Judea = _____ **(your state)**

Samaria = _____ **(your country)**

Ends of the earth = the whole earth

Jesus said you will be "fishers of men" in your city, your state, your country, and around the world. In reality, you will be a witness NO MATTER where you go.

Read "Matthew's Story."

Matthew's Story

For many years, Matthew served with Christians in one of the most dangerous parts of the world. Becoming a Christian in this almost exclusively Muslim nation was extremely dangerous.

Matthew explained, "When people come to faith in Christ, they are asked to make a list of all the unbelievers they know—which is typically just about everyone. The believers are asked to circle the names of the 10 people on the list who are least likely to kill them for becoming a Christian. After the believers complete this, they are encouraged to share the gospel as quickly as they can with each of these 10 people. That is what new believers are doing and that is why the gospel is spreading in that country."

- **In what ways is Matthew being a "fisher of men"?**

- **Would you be willing to risk your life in the same way Matthew is risking his? Why or why not?**

Most Christians today are not willing to share what they believe about Jesus with anyone. In fact, many have hardly, if ever, told someone about Jesus. Even for people who have shared the gospel at some point, most are not actively leading people around them to follow Jesus.

- **Do you agree or disagree with the previous paragraph?**

  ☐ Agree　☐ Disagree

- **Why?**

Circle the decisions you made today.

Get out of bed	**Read my Bible**	**Talk to my parents**
Complete my homework	**Get dressed**	**Text my friends**
Take a shower	**Listen to music**	**Watch television**
Study for a test	**Eat lunch**	**Clean my room**
Brush my teeth	**Tell someone about Jesus**	

- **Why did you make these decisions?**

- **How many of the decisions did you make without even thinking about them?**

- **What impact did these decisions have on you or someone around you?**

Like people all around the world, followers of Jesus are confronted with numerous decisions every day. Many of the decisions we face offer us several options—should I have cereal or pizza for breakfast? Should I take a shower now or this afternoon? Most of these decisions are not very significant, but at other times they can be life-changing.

- **How easy is it for you to make decisions? Why?**

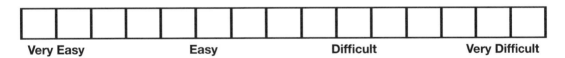

Very Easy   **Easy**   **Difficult**   **Very Difficult**

- **How do you decide what to do when you face a difficult decision?**

Everyone faces decisions, but for Christians everything takes on a different perspective because of one BIG question—**What is God's will for my life?** Before we can answer this question, we have to answer another question—**How do I know what God's will is for my life?**

I wonder though, *Do we spend more time trying to discover what God's will is for our lives than actually living out His purpose*? Let me state it this way: "Simply knowing and trusting God is far more important than searching for God's will. We want easy answers. But this is not God's will."

God's ultimate concern is not to get us from one point to another the easiest, quickest, or clearest way possible. His ultimate concern is that we know Him better and trust Him more.

- **How do you know and trust God?**

We have already discovered that being a follower of Jesus means He transforms our lives, which includes our wills. Read the words of Paul recorded in Galatians 2:20. How do these words apply to your life?

SEARCH THE SCRIPTURES

Read John 4:34 and 6:38.

- **What did Jesus say was His purpose in coming to earth?**

- **What was God's will for Jesus?**

THINK ABOUT THIS

Jesus was fully committed to doing God's will. Jesus did not let anything stop Him from the task, even though following God's will meant dying on the cross. Are you wiling to surrender total control of your life to following God's will? Are you willing to give Him EVERYTHING? Jesus will ask a lot of you, just as He asked much of His disciples.

Read Luke 9:23.

- **What did Jesus say would need to happen to be His follower?**

- **Do you have any fears about following Jesus? If so, what are they?**

I can promise you one thing—giving our lives to Jesus is never easy—but it is always worth it. God is worthy of our surrender. He is worthy of our total submission and complete obedience. Remember: He loves us as our Father.

Let me challenge you to do something this week—stop trying to find God's will for your life. Instead of asking God, "What is Your will for my life?" say, "God, I will obey Your will for my life. Whatever You ask me to do, I will do it."

Are you ready? If so, tell God, but be careful. Don't make any promises you are not willing to keep.

Think about how things change. Check *Then* if the action took place 50 years ago. Check *Now* if the action can be done today. (You may check both.)

Then		Now
	Write letters, place them in envelopes, stamp the envelopes, and mail the letters	
	Search the Internet	
	Hear news from other countries almost instantly	
	Text, receive instant messages	
	Watch events as they happen	
	Read encyclopedias, research books	
	Fly across the country in a few hours	
	Travel by ship	

- **What are some changes that have happened in your life?**

- **How have these changes impacted your life?**

- **In what ways did Jesus impact the lives of His disciples while He was here on earth?**

▶ SEARCH THE SCRIPTURES

Jesus' impact did not stop once He returned to heaven. Read each Scripture passage and match it to the person it describes.

Acts 9:3-6	**Ananias**
Acts 9:10-19	**Peter**
Acts 10:9-22	**Saul**

The Book of Acts (as well as the rest of the New Testament) tells us how Jesus impacted the lives of people. Sometimes Jesus did things Himself, while other times He chose to work through people. Jesus is still working through people! He wants to use His followers to impact the world. The question we must answer is, "Are we willing to allow Jesus to use us?"

- **How will you respond to this question: "Am I willing to allow Jesus to use me to impact my world?"**

I know as a preteen you may have no clue about what job you will have when you grow up. You probably have not given any thought about whom you will marry, or if you will get married at all. You are dealing with acne, peer-pressure, school tests, report cards, and other issues. Relax, God knows and understands what you are going through, but He doesn't want you to use these things as excuses. God does not want you to say, "I'll serve Him when I get older." He wants to use you right now, right where you are!

Make a list of five people you interact with on a daily basis. Beside each name, write one or two ways this person impacts you, either in a positive or negative way. In the third column, write a way you impact each person.

Person	How the Person Impacts Me	How I Impact the Person

Whether we admit it or not, we are all impacted by other people. Think about the impact Jesus and the disciples had on people. In what ways did Jesus change the lives of people? What did He allow to stop Him from being committed to following God's plan for His life? Nothing!

Here's some great news. God does not expect you to be perfect. He is not waiting on you to get your life straightened out before He can use you. He is willing to straighten your life out! He wants you to allow Him to work in your life. Are you willing to let Him do so?

I want to challenge you to do something different today. Stand in front of a mirror and look at yourself. What do you see? Do you see someone God can use? Do you see yourself as God sees you? Now, say out loud, "God, I want You to use me." Please, don't say this if you don't mean it, but if you are really fully committed to following Jesus, say these words. Repeat them again. Again. One more time. Say it like you really mean it.

Have you ever tried to walk across a room in pitch darkness? What happened when you discovered your book bag in the middle of the floor? Did you fall? Did you hurt your big toe?

Sometimes we face obstacles in our lives. If we are not careful, obstacles can keep us from doing what we started to do. Have you ever thought about how you can be an obstacle?

On Day 1 of this week's study, I made the statement that simply knowing God and obeying His commands is far more important than trying to identify His will for our lives. One of the reasons this is true is because following Jesus means surrendering our wills in submission to His will—it means our lives are literally His life. We get out of His way and let Him work through us.

►SEARCH THE SCRIPTURES

Read Matthew 28:19-20 and Acts 1:7-8.

- **What do these verses say about God's will for the world?**

God's will is for everyone from every nation, tribe, language, and people to be redeemed through His grace and for His glory.

God's will is for the followers of Jesus to make disciples. That is our purpose. That is how we participate in Jesus' work of spreading His kingdom in this world.

- **How does it make you feel to know Jesus wants you to make disciples?**

redeem
to pay a price in order to get something back from someone else

►THINK ABOUT THIS

We talked about how being a follower of Jesus is more than just knowing who Jesus is. He wants us to experience Him—to really get to know Him. Once we know Jesus on a more personal level, we want to tell people about Him so they can become His followers too!

Write down five facts you know about Jesus.

1.

2.

3.

4.

5.

- **How did you learn these facts? Does knowing this information make a difference in your life? Why or why not?**

- **In what ways have you gotten to know Jesus on a more personal level (more than just knowing facts about Him)?**

- **How has getting to know Jesus on a more personal level impacted your life?**

- **Do you desire for other people to know Jesus and to have the same type of relationship that you have? Why or why not? What are you willing to do to help people follow Jesus?**

The great news is that God has not asked us to do something that He is not willing to help us accomplish. We have a guarantee that our efforts and sacrifices will accomplish what God wants. The Bible has promised that will happen. Today we will look at the promises in the Old Testament; tomorrow we will examine the New Testament.

Read Genesis 1:27-28.

- **What did God instruct Adam and Eve to do?**

God wanted His relationship with Adam and Eve to grow. However, we know Adam and Eve disobeyed God. As a result of their disobedience, their relationship with God changed, creating a separation from God. God still loved Adam and Eve though, and did not abandon them. He continued to work through people.

Read the verses listed and fill in the information.

VERSES	WHOM DID GOD SPEAK TO?	WHAT DID GOD TELL THE PERSON?
GENESIS 12:1-3		
GENESIS 26:1-6		
GENESIS 28:10-15		

God's will is also found in the praises of His people. Read Psalm 67:1-4.

- **What does this psalm say about "the nations"?**

The prophets (people who spoke God's word to the people) also spoke about God's plan. Read Isaiah 66:18-19 and Habakkuk 2:14.

The more we understand God's will for the world and submit to Him, the more we will understand why He will not hide His will from us. God's desire is for us to know and follow His will—to make disciples of all nations.

- **Do you care about the people around the world? How can you help people in different countries know how they can have a relationship with Jesus?**

Locate a map of the world. Randomly place your finger on a country. Pray for the people living in that country. Do this several times, praying for people in different countries. Ask God to help you be willing to do whatever you need to do to tell people about Jesus.

Yesterday we learned about getting out of the way and allowing God to use us. We also discovered some Old Testament passages that tell about God's plan to reach people in every nation. Today, let's discover how the New Testament reveals God's plan for reaching people.

SEARCH THE SCRIPTURES

Yesterday we read Matthew 28:19-20. These verses are called "The Great Commission" because Jesus challenged His disciples to go into all the world and tell people about Him. Read the definition of *commission*. Read Matthew 24:12-14. Jesus said His gospel will be preached to the whole world. In Acts 1:8, Jesus told the disciples they would be His witnesses around the world.

Read Revelation 7:9-10.

- **Where did these people come from?**

- **What do these verses tell us about the purpose of Jesus' followers?**

> ## commission
> an order or instruction granting the power to perform various acts or duties

THINK ABOUT THIS

God's will is to create, call, save, and bless His people so they can spread His grace and glory to others. God is not hiding His will waiting on someone to find it. He tells us His will so we can follow it. We don't have to wonder about God's will. We were created to follow it. **We don't need to ask God to show us His will; instead, we need to ask God to help us do what He wants us to do.**

I know you are probably thinking, *I am not Simon Peter, Andrew, James, John, or one of the other 12 original disciples of Jesus. How can I tell people around the world about Jesus?*

Let's explore this question a little deeper. Read the following sentences very carefully. The answer to your question has very little to do with you and a lot to do with the Holy Spirit. God wants you to experience His will so much that He actually lives inside you in order to accomplish it.

- **What ideas come to mind when you hear the name *Holy Spirit*?**

As followers of Jesus, God ties our lives together with Jesus by putting His Spirit inside of us. Only through the Holy Spirit do we find the power necessary for making disciples.

Read Luke 24:46-49.

- **Whom did Jesus say would be sent?**

Read Acts 2:1-4.

- **How do you think you would have reacted if you were in the room when God sent the Holy Spirit?**

The Bible makes it very clear that a specific type of power is needed in order for us to obey Jesus' command to make disciples. We do not have this power apart from God—this power comes from God. The Holy Spirit is God's Spirit.

- **How does it make you feel to know the Holy Spirit (God's Spirit) lives in you?**

- **In what ways do you feel empowered to make disciples because of the Holy Spirit living in you?**

As followers of Jesus empowered by the Holy Spirit, we have a responsibility to live as witnesses. We have a responsibility to tell about who Jesus is, what Jesus did, and how Jesus saves.

empower
to give someone the abiilty or authority to do something

- **Are you willing to accept this responsibility? Why or why not?**

Read Acts 4:31.

- **What did the people do after being filled with the Holy Spirit?**

Read Acts 9:17-20.

- **What did Saul do after being filled with the Holy Spirit?**

These are just two places the Bible talks about people being filled with the Holy Spirit. The filling of the Holy Spirit in people's lives is clearly linked to a specific purpose: the verbal sharing of God's Word, which is the accomplishment of God's will.

Even after Jesus returned to heaven, He continued to work by placing the Holy Spirit in the lives of His followers, empowering them to proclaim the gospel to people.

As followers of Jesus, we have the same purpose today! We have the Holy Spirit living in us to fulfill God's purpose of telling people about Jesus.

I often hear Christians say, "I share the gospel when the Holy Spirit leads me." There is some truth in that statement. We want to be led by the Holy Spirit in everything we do. At the same time, we need to remember that the Spirit lives in us for the purpose of spreading the gospel. Since believers have the Holy Spirit living in them, they can know they should tell people about Jesus. Believers should open their mouths and talk about the life, death, and resurrection of Jesus. When we do this, we will be carrying out the purpose of Jesus' presence in us.

- **How often do you tell people about Jesus?**

☐ **Every day**

☐ **Once a week**

☐ **Once a month**

☐ **I have never told anyone about Jesus**

☐ **(Other)** _____

- **What prevents you from telling people about Jesus?**

God has given us a gospel to believe, a Spirit to empower, and a language to speak for a purpose.

- **Do you believe this? What difference is it making in your life?**

Confess times you did not tell people about Jesus. Ask God to forgive you. Thank Him for sending the Holy Spirit to live in you. Ask God to help you be like the disciples and tell people everywhere you go about Jesus.

I live in the southern part of the United States. For a lot of people here, college football is a big part of their lives. People paint their bodies, wear crazy outfits, and spend hours watching and cheering on their favorite teams.

- **Do you have a favorite team? Why is that team your favorite?**

- **Have you ever tried to convince someone to cheer for your team? What happened?**

After watching people cheer for their favorite football team, I wonder, *If we are so excited about our sports teams and willing to get someone to cheer for our team, why are we not so excited about telling people about Jesus?*

SEARCH THE SCRIPTURES

Read Acts 26.

The events in Acts 26 help us see that even though Paul had been arrested and was having to defend his actions, he still used the situations in his life to tell people about Jesus.

- **What did you find most amazing about Paul's testimony before King Agrippa?**

- **How would you have responded to King Agrippa's question, "Are you trying to get me to become a Christian?"**

THINK ABOUT THIS

Do you remember what we said God's purpose for our lives is? God's purpose is for us to tell people about Jesus all around the world. Let's examine three aspects of God's purpose: who, how, and when.

WHO?

Do you remember the story of Ayan that we read on the very first day of our study? She lived every day knowing that at any moment she could be killed because she had become a follower of Jesus. You most likely will not be killed because you're a Christian, but I know many Christians living in different parts of the world who daily put their lives in jeopardy.

Take a minute and write down the names of some people you know who are not Christians.

-
-
-
-

-
-
-
-

Spend a few minutes praying for each person whose name you wrote down. Ask God to help each person know how much He loves him.

HOW?

We have opportunities to tell people about Jesus every day. I understand you may be afraid. We all have fears that come up when we think about telling someone about Jesus. We may fear offending someone, saying the wrong thing, being rejected, or someone making fun of us. For some of us, even knowing how to start the conversation is difficult.

- **What fears keep you from telling people about Jesus?**

Fears are only a sign that we are forgetting who we are. We are followers of Jesus. Remember what we learned—we have been crucified with Him; we no longer live, but Christ lives in us. He has given us the Holy Spirit to help us. Without Jesus, we have a reason to fear, but with Him, we have reason to believe He will help us.

Here's a personal challenge from me to you—pray every morning that God will give you grace as you attempt to tell people about Jesus. Pray for boldness—for the ability to overcome fear. Throughout the day, look for opportunities to tell people about Jesus.

- **Will you accept my challenge? Why or why not?**

WHEN?

Think about all the places you will go today. Who will you see today? What do you know about these people? How many of these people know you are a Christian? Have you told any of these people what you believe about Jesus? Why or why not?

- **In what ways can you begin a conversation with people about Jesus?**

Write out a conversation between you and someone you can tell about Jesus. How will you respond if the person says she wants to know more about becoming a Christian? How will you respond if the person says she is not interested in knowing about Jesus?

God knows exactly where we are 24 hours a day, 7 days a week. He expects us to be witnesses everywhere we go. Ask God to help you have courage to speak to the people you see.

As we identify the *who*, think through the *how*, and plan the *when*, we cannot forget the *why*—everyone around us is a sinner needing to know Jesus as Savior and Lord.

This week we talked about God's purpose for our lives.

- **How do you feel knowing God has a plan for your life?**

- **Did you discover anything new about God's plan?**

- **Are you committed to following God's plan? Why or why not?**

Let's start following God's plan.

SEARCH THE SCRIPTURES

Read Acts 4:1-12.

- **How did the religious leaders respond to Peter and John?**

- **Why do you think about 5,000 people responded to Peter and John's teaching?**

- **By whose power did Peter and John say they taught?**

This is just one story of followers telling people what they believed about Jesus. As a result of Peter and John's willingness to speak up, about 5,000 people believed what they heard about Jesus. The religious leaders did not agree with Peter and John's teachings.

Even today, not everyone will agree with what we say about Jesus. Some people will try to make us stop telling about Jesus, and others will make fun of us and say we are wasting our time. We can know God wants us to tell people about Jesus and our purpose is to do so.

THINK ABOUT THIS

The more we tell people about Jesus, the easier it can become. Ask your parents if you can tell them what you know about Jesus. Spend a few minutes talking with your parents. Ask them to pretend to be someone who does not know about Jesus. Invite your parents to ask questions to agree with what you say, and want to know more about Jesus. Also ask your parents to pretend they do not want to know about Jesus. How will you deal with their responses?

Now, put into practice what we talked about this week. Share what you know about Jesus with someone, then complete the following chart.

PLACE I TOLD SOMEONE ABOUT JESUS	
WHO I TOLD ABOUT JESUS	
HOW THE PERSON RESPONDED	
GOOD PARTS OF MY SHARING ABOUT JESUS	
THINGS I NEED TO WORK ON WHEN SHARING ABOUT JESUS	
WHAT GOD DID WHILE I SHARED ABOUT JESUS	

Each time you have the opportunity to tell someone about Jesus, make notes of your experience. Keep your notes and look back through them. In what ways is God using you to reach the people around the world?

Pray for the person you told about Jesus.

THE CHURCH

For the last four weeks we explored what it means to be a follower of Jesus.

- **What would you say if someone asked you, "What does it mean to be a follower of Jesus?"**

- **What have you learned that has challenged your thinking about being a follower of Jesus?**

- **Are you still committed to following Jesus? Why or why not?**

We examined the costs and rewards of following Jesus. In Week 2, Day 5, I mentioned what some other religious groups say about Jesus' death. We discovered how following Jesus transforms our wants and needs, and ultimately our purpose for living. We have a better understanding of what it means to delight in Jesus, and how we should obey God's will.

Now let's look at the church. What does it mean for a follower of Jesus to participate in the church?

To be a follower of Jesus is to be a part of His church. When we die to ourselves and Jesus lives in us, God brings us together into a family of faith. As a family, we worship, serve, give, protect, and care for one another.

church
a building where people meet to worship God
a group of Christians who meet together to pray, tell others about Jesus, worship God, learn from the Bible, meet the needs of others, and encourage one another

- **Who are some members of your faith family?**

- **How does it make you feel to know other followers of Jesus serve, give, protect, and care for you?**

- **In what ways do you serve, give, protect, and care for other people in your church?**

- **What do you enjoy most about worshiping with other followers of Jesus? Why?**

Read "The Preacher Said."

The Preacher Said

The room was packed full of people, and the preacher had everyone's undivided attention. "I would like everyone to bow your head and close your eyes," he said. Everyone did so. The preacher continued, "Tonight, I want to call you to put your faith in God. Tonight, I am urging you to begin a personal relationship with Jesus for the first time in your life."

"Let me be clear," the preacher continued, "I'm not inviting you to join the church. I'm just inviting you to come to Christ." As he passionately pleaded for personal decisions, a large number of people stood up and walked down the aisles to make a commitment to Christ.

- **How would you respond to the preacher's invitation? Why?**

Honestly, I felt conflicted about what was taking place. I was excited so many people responded to the Holy Spirit. I rejoiced that men and women expressed their desire to follow Jesus.

Yet, there was a problem. The people walking down the aisles had been misled. They had been told it is possible to make a commitment to Jesus apart from a commitment to the church—something I knew to be untrue.

Here's the truth—it is biblically impossible to follow Jesus apart from joining His church.

- **Do you agree or disagree with this statement? Why?**

  ☐ Agree ☐ Disagree

Respond to these statements.

  Joining a church makes a person a Christian.

  ☐ Agree ☐ Disagree

  Becoming a follower of Jesus means you join your life with other believers.

  ☐ Agree ☐ Disagree

Hopefully you checked "Disagree" for the first statement. Joining a church does not make a person a Christian. Did you check "Agree" for the second statement? I hope so. To become a follower of Jesus means that you commit your life to His church.

Read Hebrews 10:24-25.

- **What does verse 25 tell us to do?**

- **Why did the writer of Hebrews caution the believers about not meeting together?**

▶ THINK ABOUT THIS

- **When you think about being a part of the church, what comes to your mind?**

Read both of the definitions of *church* (page 77).

- **Which definition do you think of most when you hear the word *church*? Why?**

- **How does the second definition differ from most people's view of church?**

- **How involved are you in your church? Check all the things you do.**

___ **Attend Bible study**	___ **Help other people**
___ **Participate in worship**	___ **Encourage other people**
___ **Sing in choir**	___ **Serve other people**
___ **Tithe**	___ **Other:** _____
___ **Pray for other people**	___ **Other:** _____

Many people today do not like the church. Does this surprise you? What should surprise us is the number of Christians who have chosen to stop being a part of the church.

- **What are some reasons people do not attend church (the building)?**

Some people have even said, "I love Jesus, but I cannot stand the church." When I hear people say this, I want to ask them, "How can you love Jesus without loving the church?" The church is the body of Christ. How can you love Jesus without loving His body? To answer these questions, only two words are needed—YOU CAN'T!

In the space below, draw a picture of your church.

Look at your drawing. Did you draw a building or people? Why?

Take time to thank God for your church (both the building and the body of Christ). Ask God to work through your church to help more people learn about becoming followers of Jesus.

How do you feel about vocabulary lessons in school? Do you enjoy learning new words, learning to spell them, discovering if they are adjectives, nouns, verbs, or other parts of speech? Let's learn two words and how they apply to the church.

Match the words with the correct definitions.

Extra biblical

something that adds to the truth of God's Word; something that is often connected to the Bible but does not have its source in the Bible

Unbiblical

something that undercuts the truth of God's Word—a concept or idea that is in disagreement with the story of the Bible

Did you draw lines straight across from the words to the definitions? You should have. The correct definitions are beside the words.

You are probably wondering, *Why are we studying vocabulary? I thought this was a Bible study.* You are correct, but I want to emphasize these words because they are current misunderstandings about the church.

SEARCH THE SCRIPTURES

Read 1 Corinthians 12.

Throughout the New Testament, the church is described as the body of Christ. Followers of Jesus are parts of the body. We each have a purpose.

- **What is your purpose in the body of Christ?**

- **Do you feel like you are fulfilling your purpose in the body? Why or why not?**

THINK ABOUT THIS

In 1 Corinthians 12, Paul described "the body of Christ" to help us understand that the church is made up of individual human beings, with different goals and desires, yet we all have one thing in common—to live in God's will.

- **In what ways does the church function as a team?**

- **What happens when a church does not function as a team?**

The term *body of Christ* refers to both the Christians all around the world and the local church in your community. The Greek word *ekklesia* (EK klih SEE uh) (church) is used 114 times in the New Testament. At least 90 of these references are used to refer to a local church (group of believers).

Read these verses and match them to the church the verses address.

Acts 11:22

Romans 16:3-5

1 Corinthians 1:2

The Corinth church

This church met at Priscilla and Aquila's home

The Jerusalem church

In all the letters Paul wrote to churches, he never addressed any of them to specific individuals in the church. This showed Paul's desire for all individuals to be joined together as one. The church is a group of people who share the life of Jesus with each other day by day, and week by week. When someone is in need, the other members of the body help. When someone is happy, the other members are happy. When someone is sad, the other members are sad.

Look back at the definitions of *extra biblical* and *unbiblical*.

- **How would you associate these words with the word *church*?**

- **Are followers of Jesus guilty of adding extra biblical or unbiblical concepts to our understanding of church? In what ways?**

The church is the body of Christ living and active in the world; it is a community of Christians who love one another and desire for each other to know and grow in Jesus.

Pray for the leadership of your church. Ask God to help your pastor, staff, deacons, and other leaders be sensitive to the real meaning of the word *church*. Ask God to help you understand you are a part of the body of Christ and help you know what part you are to play in the body.

Think back to the last time you disobeyed your parents. What happened? Did your parents discipline you? What do you learn from your discipline?

Read the definition of *discipline*.

Many times we think of discipline as a negative part of life— we misbehave so our parents discipline us. In what ways do these individuals need discipline?

discipline
strict training that corrects or strengthens habits or ways of acting that are acquired through practice

Chef	**Author**	**Student**
Athlete	**Actor**	**Doctor**
Scientist	**Judge**	**Teacher**

For a person to be a great athlete, he must discipline himself to eat the right foods, exercise every day, learn all he can about his sport, know his equipment, learn about his competition, and give his body time to rest. Sounds like a lot to be a great athlete, doesn't it?

What about us as followers of Jesus? What types of things do we need to do to be disciplined? Reading the Bible, attending church, praying, and telling other people about Jesus are all disciplines we need in our lives.

What would you do if you knew someone in your church was teaching things that were not true? Would you talk with him about his teachings? What if someone was living in ways that did not please and honor God—what would you do?

While having lunch with another pastor, I told him our church was going to start a process of church discipline and help people live in ways that honor God. The pastor said to me, "I would love to hear how that goes. Give me a call in a few weeks if you are still at your church."

I am still at the same church, and I am sure this is the direction God wants my church to move. I think we need to help people when they are not living in ways that please and honor God. However, I know that many people do not have positive thoughts about the idea of church discipline. This is an issue that must be addressed very carefully. Let's see what the Bible says about it.

Read Matthew 18:15-20.

- **What does verse 15 say to do when someone does something against you?**

- **What should you do if the person does not listen to you?**

► THINK ABOUT THIS

Jesus wants His followers to be committed to Him. He does not want people to believe or teach things that are not true. He does not want us to live like non-Christians. He wants us to be different. When people are not living in ways that honor Jesus, we should lovingly confront them.

- **Has anyone ever pointed out something you were doing that was not honoring to Jesus? How did you feel about being confronted by someone?**

- **How did your actions change?**

Read James 5:19-20.

- **What keeps you from lovingly correcting someone's actions or helping him see that his actions are not pleasing to Jesus?**

- **According to James 5:19-20, what are the benefits of lovingly correcting someone's actions?**

Let me give you a word of warning—be careful before you start pointing out things other people are doing wrong. We must remember that we need help as well. We need people in our lives who will hold us accountable to live as followers of Jesus. We must be willing to listen to what people say, examine our lives, and change what needs to be changed.

I know you are wondering, *Won't some people leave the church if we start disciplining them?* Most likely some people will, however we need to remember that the church is Jesus' body and He wants us to honor God.

Take time to really examine your life. If someone saw everything you did, said, thought, or how you acted today, what would she say about your commitment to Jesus? How would you feel if she disciplined you for these things?

- **Have you ever been a part of a club? If so, what kind?**

- **Did your club have any rules for membership? If so, what were they?**

- **How did you feel being a part of the club?**

Being a follower of Jesus means we are a part of His body, the church. I want us to explore an area that I feel is becoming an issue for the church. Before we jump in to this discussion, let me tell you about an experience I had when I was around 15 years old.

Read "My First Date."

My First Date

Up to this time in my life I had not had much success with girlfriends. OK–honestly, I had not had any success–until this one girl came to a camp I was attending. Word got around camp that this girl thought I was cute. A little while later we started dating, which consisted of us talking on the phone every day and spending time together.

For a while everything was going great, until one night I decided I did not want to talk on the phone any longer. In fact, I decided I did not want to continue our relationship at all. I told the girl that I had a lot of things going on in my life—I told her that God, my family, and my schoolwork were more important to me than her.

Yep, you read that right. I told her my schoolwork was more important than her. Needless to say, my first dating experience did not last very long.

I know you are only a preteen and probably don't have much, if any, experience dating. But let's think about this issue today.

- **When you hear the word *dating*, what comes to your mind?**

- **What do your friends mean when they say, "I'm dating someone"?**

You may be wondering, *Why are we talking about dating in relation to the church? What does this have to do with me as a preteen?* Let me share my thoughts and concerns about the church. I am seeing a trend develop in our Christian culture that is often referred to as "dating the church." In today's world, people have developed the practice of moving from one church to another based on what the church offers. Many times these decisions are based on the style of music, the style of the pastor, ministries offered, the time of the worship services, and so forth.

I have even had people ask me, "Why do I need to commit to a local church?" I respond by saying that as a follower of Jesus we need to spend time with other followers. We should value our relationships with Jesus and His followers.

- **What does it mean to be a member of a local church?**

- **Are you a member of a local church? Why or why not?**

- **If you are a member of a local church, how did you become a member?**

For many people, the idea of "dating the church" is a desire to avoid having to commit themselves to a specific body of believers. I listed some reasons people give for moving from one church to another. What other reasons can you think of?

 **SEARCH THE SCRIPTURES**

Read Acts 2:37-47.

Peter preached about the forgiveness provided through Jesus. Peter told the people to repent and be baptized. According to verse 41 about 3,000 people responded to Peter's teaching.

- **What does verse 42 say the people did?**

Verses 44-47 tell us more about what the believers did. They met together! They ate together! They shared everything they owned! They praised God together!

If we are not careful, we can miss the importance of church membership expressed in the New Testament. The writers of the New Testament almost always assumed followers of Jesus were a part of a local group of believers. Paul wrote his letters to the churches at Corinth, Rome, Philippi, Colossae, and others. We never see the New Testament writers address followers of Jesus who did not belong to a local church.

If you do not regularly worship with other followers of Jesus, let me encourage you to begin doing so. I hope you see that Jesus expects His followers to be a part of a local church.

Pray for your church. Ask God to help your church become a place where people feel loved by one another and by God.

(I don't want to end today's session without telling you how my first dating experience ended. Thankfully, I had an opportunity to get to know this girl all over again. In fact, things got to the point that we became best friends and decided to get married. The girl I met at camp was Heather, my wife.)

How would you respond if someone made these comments to you?

Going to church is a waste of time.

I don't know why you go to church. What can you learn at church that you cannot learn at home?

The people who go to church do not live differently than people who do not go to church.

SEARCH THE SCRIPTURES

Read Ephesians 4:1-6.

- **What do you find most interesting about these verses? Why?**

- **How do these verses say a follower of Jesus is to live?**

Paul wrote these words to the church at Ephesus. He challenged them to walk worthy of the calling they had received—to be followers of Jesus. Apply these verses to your life. Read aloud the verses, inserting your name in place of the word *you*.

- **Do these verses challenge you in the way you are living?**

- **Are you living out these actions? Why or why not?**

Paul wanted the followers in Ephesus, as well as us, to know that as members of the church we not only belong to Jesus, we belong to each other. We all have different backgrounds, different personalities, different likes and dislikes, but we all form one church. Our connecting bond between one another is our relationship with Jesus.

Read Ephesians 4:11-13.

- **What responsibilities did God give people?**

- **What is the purpose of these responsibilities?**

- **Who fulfills these responsibilities in your church?**

Read Ephesians 4:14-16.

Paul stated that everything is to be done in love. We speak the truth in love and build up one another in love. Jesus taught that speaking the truth in love is the most important part of church body.

Read John 13:35.

- **How are we as followers of Jesus to respond to one another?**

- **In what ways have you felt loved in your church?**

- **In what ways have you made someone else feel loved?**

THINK ABOUT THIS

Let me share with you my definition of a local church.

The church is a local body of baptized believers joined together in biblical leadership to grow in the likeness of Jesus and express the love of Jesus to each other and around the world.

- **Do you agree or disagree with my definition? Why?**

| | Agree | | Disagree

Do you want to be a part of this type of community? Take a few minutes and reflect on these three questions:

Are you committed to a local church?

Which local church should you commit to?

How can you serve as a member of your church?

Pray for the leaders of your church. Ask God to help them lead the church in ways that please and honor God.

Yesterday we read some verses from the Book of Ephesians that talked about people having different responsibilities in the church. I want to take this thought a little bit further and talk about how you as a preteen can serve in your church.

Take two minutes and list all the ways people serve in your church.

Look back over your list. Circle several ways you would like to serve.

- **Why did you select these ways?**

- **In what ways are you currently serving?**

Read the definition of *service*.

Have you ever thought of yourself as a servant? As followers of Jesus we are to serve other people. Read the last part of Galatians 5:13. What does this verse say about our attitude in serving others?

service
the occupation or function of serving or working as a servant

SEARCH THE SCRIPTURES

Read John 13:1-11.

- **In what way did Jesus serve the disciples?**

- **How do you think the disciples felt as Jesus washed their feet? Why?**

- **Why do you think none of the disciples volunteered to wash the others' feet?**

Jesus wanted to show His followers what it meant to serve others. Usually the job of washing feet was a servant's task. Jesus assumed the role of the servant and cleaned the feet of His followers. Jesus showed His followers should be willing to do whatever needs to be done.

THINK ABOUT THIS

Look back at the list of ways people serve in your church. Did you list dishwasher, custodian, or plumber? What type of actions do these jobs include? Many times people want to serve in ways people can see them serving. While these tasks need to be accomplished as well, someone has to clean the toilets, vacuum the floors, and empty the trash cans. Someone needs to make sure dishes are washed and put away.

- **How would you respond if someone asked you to vacuum the floors? Clean the toilets? Empty the trash?**

- **When was the last time you volunteered to do something at church without someone having to ask you?**

- **Have you ever done something without someone asking you to do it? How did it make you feel to know you helped without anyone even knowing you did something?**

As we discovered this week, being a member of a local church is very important. However, God does not want us to watch as other people do everything. We have all been given gifts to use to serve God. How will you use your gifts?

Pray for opportunities to serve this week.

If you had the ability to look 10 years into the future, what would you hope to see? Would you have completed school? Would you be married? Where would you be living? What type of car would you drive?

- **What do you want out of life?**

- **What do you hope to experience as a follower of Jesus?**

I'll tell you what I want: I want to be a part of a people who really believe we have God's Spirit in us to help all people know about Him. I want to be a part of a group of people who are gladly sacrificing our pleasures, pursuits, and possessions of this world because we are living for the treasures in the world to come. I want to be a part of a group of people who have given up every earthly ambition in favor of one eternal desire: to see disciples made and churches multiplied from our houses to our communities to our cities and to the nations.

This kind of movement involves everyone of us being actively involved. In this type of situation no one sits on the sidelines and watches. Everyone participates. This is God's design for His church. As disciples of Jesus we must not settle for anything less.

Can you imagine what our world would look like if all of Jesus' followers began to prayerfully, humbly, simply, and intentionally make disciples? What if every one of us as followers of Jesus really started helping people know how to follow Jesus? This is the way God designed for people to hear and experience His love. This is the life God has planned for every child of His—to enjoy His grace as we extend His glory to every group of people in the world.

What about you? As we finish this study together, what do you want?

At the beginning of our study we read about Jesus' calling of the first four disciples. Read Matthew 4:18-22. Jesus' words changed the lives of these four men.

I think it is appropriate, then, that we end this study by exploring the last words Jesus spoke to His disciples recorded in the Book of Matthew. We usually refer to these words as "The Great Commission" (we talked about this in Week 4).

Read Matthew 28:18-20.

- **What commands did Jesus give His disciples?**

- **How did Jesus encourage His disciples?**

These verses are familiar to most Christians, and they should be the basis of all of our decisions, however, we too often forget these verses. Do you agree with me that tragically The Great Commission represents one of the best-known and most-ignored passages in the Bible? I long for that to change. I long for these words to be applied to our lives as disciples of Jesus. I long for these words to be the center of EVERYTHING we do.

Over the next few days we will explore three parts of Matthew 28:18-20. These parts include:

Believe Jesus' authority

Obey Jesus' commands

Depend on Jesus' presence

BELIEVE JESUS' AUTHORITY

Suppose you and your best friend are riding your bikes to the grocery store. Clearly posted outside the store are signs reading, "No skateboards, bicycles, or roller blades allowed on the sidewalks." You ignore the signs and continue to ride your bike. A police officer motions for you to come to him. What would you do?

authority
a person looked to as an expert; power to influence the behavior of others

Most likely you would get off of your bike and walk over to the police officer. Why? Because the police officer has the authority to make you get off of your bike—and the authority to call your parents if you refuse. His authority compels you to obedience.

Read the definition of *authority* (page 94).

- **Who are the primary sources of authority in your life? Circle all that apply.**

Parents	**Friends**	**Siblings**
Teachers	**Pastor**	**Grandparents**
Police officers	**Principal**	

- **How do you respond to people who have authority over you? Why?**

SEARCH THE SCRIPTURES

Imagine you are one of Jesus' disciples. You have walked with Him, listened to Him teach about God, watched Him heal people, even knew He had been crucified and raised from the dead. Now you and the 10 other disciples (Judas has killed himself) are gathered together again. When Jesus appears you begin to worship Him. Jesus comes near to tell you that all authority has been given to Him. He says, "Go make disciples of every nation."

- **How would you feel if you were with Jesus at this moment?**

Jesus' instruction (commission) to the disciples was an important moment in history because it set a precedent for the future—for everything the disciples would accomplish after His return to heaven. Jesus' claim to have all authority in heaven and on earth was also an important connection to the past. Specifically, it connected Jesus with a major prophecy delivered hundreds of years earlier by the prophet Daniel.

Read Daniel 7:13-14.

- **What words or phrases do you find most interesting in these verses? Why?**

- **How do Daniel's words relate to Jesus' life?**

Jesus came to fulfill God's plan for the world—God wants to redeem (save) every person on earth. Jesus' commission was not about one group of people. His commission is for ALL people. His authority was not for one group of people, but for ALL people. That includes you and me!

Read these Scripture passages and match them with the correct descriptions of Jesus' authority.

Matthew 8:23-27	**Jesus has authority to forgive sins.**
Matthew 9:1-8	**Jesus has authority over death.**
Matthew 28:1-10	**Jesus has authority over the winds and the sea.**

Do you believe Jesus has authority? If so, your life will reflect your belief in His authority. To be a disciple of Jesus means we live under His authority—we surrender every part of our lives to Him. If we surrender to His authority, we must pay attention to what He said next in Matthew 28:19, "Therefore, go ...." (We will explore this tomorrow.)

Evaluate your life. Do you really believe Jesus has authority? If so, ask Him to help you live under His authority. If you do not believe Jesus has authority, confess it to Him. Ask Him to help you understand His authority and how to live under it.

- **How many people do you know? In the next two minutes, write down the names of everyone you know.**

How many names did you write down? Did you know there are literally billions of people around the world who do not believe the gospel? Some of these people live in our communities; many of them live in Africa, Northern India, China, and every other country around the world. Some of these people have heard the gospel message, but rejected it; many have never even heard the good news of salvation.

Every person in the world has one thing in common—Jesus is the only One who can save them from their sins. Therefore, we must go and make the gospel known.

SEARCH THE SCRIPTURES

Read 1 Timothy 2:1-4 and 2 Peter 3:9.

- **What do these verses say to you concerning telling people about Jesus?**

- **What is God's plan for all people?**

We have two reasons for telling people about Jesus. First, because God loves everyone and wants everyone to receive His gift of salvation. Second, we must tell people about Jesus because He is worthy of honor, glory, and praise. We tell people about Jesus and help them become His followers because there are billions of people in the world who are robbing Jesus of the glory due to Him as Lord. Because Jesus is worthy, we work to tell other people about Him.

- **How does knowing what God wants you to do impact your actions and decisions?**

- **Look back at the names you listed at the beginning of today's study. Circle the names of the people who are not followers of Jesus. List specific ways you can tell these people about Jesus.**

- **In what ways do you bring honor, glory, and praise to Jesus?**

When I think of The Great Commission, I remember a small group of Christians I had the pleasure of spending time with in a predominantly Muslim country. These Christians have a successful business that employs Muslim men and women. Through the business, the owners love people and lead them to become followers of Jesus.

My friends start by sharing the gospel with their employees. They must be careful because this can lead to them being persecuted or even killed. In every conversation, business dealing, meal, and meeting, they look for ways to speak about who God is, how God loves, what God is doing in the world, and what God has done for them through Jesus.

Not every conversation leads to telling about Jesus, but their prayer is that God will give them the opportunities to help people know who Jesus is and how the people can have a relationship with Him. The great news is that it's working! Because my friends care for the people who work for them, they have earned the right to be heard. Because my friends are willing to proclaim the gospel, many of the people who hear them are experiencing salvation.

- **Think of all the people you know. Who does a good job of talking about the gospel in her everyday life?**

- **Who have you recently told about Jesus? How did the person respond?**

As I think about my friends who are willing to risk their lives to tell people about Jesus, I wonder, *Why don't we all do this? What if God has placed every one of us in different locations with different jobs and different gifts around different people for the purpose of making disciples?*

Are you ready for an eye-opening thought? In truth, that is the way God has called us to live.

Yesterday we read Matthew 28:18-20. Reread these verses.

Are these verses a ____ suggestion   ____ request   ____ command?

Hopefully you checked **command**.

You are probably wondering, *How do I actually go about making disciples?* Let's explore several steps to accomplishing this.

Go — The Bible does not tell us to sit and wait on people to come to us. We are to live as followers of Jesus in our families, communities, schools, sporting events, and so on. As we go, we are to share about Jesus as we love, care for, and encourage people.

Tell — We can tell what God has done for us as we talk about the difficulties we face and how God helps us.

- **What do your friends know about your relationship with Jesus?**

- **What can your friends learn about Jesus based on how you react to situations?**

Teach — Making followers of Jesus involves more than just leading people to trust Jesus as Savior and Lord. Making followers of Jesus means teaching people to follow Jesus. One of the first areas of teaching people to follow Jesus is baptism. We baptize new followers because doing so symbolizes their identification with Jesus.

- **What emotions did you experience when you were baptized?**

- **In what ways can you teach people what it means to follow Jesus?**

For us to be followers of Jesus we must make disciples. We must be willing to share the Word of God with people who need to hear it, as well as be willing to teach the ways of God to those who wish to follow Him.

Pray for opportunities to tell people what you believe about Jesus. Ask God to help you teach people how to become followers of Jesus.

Have you ever thought about all the people you are related to? Complete the family tree.

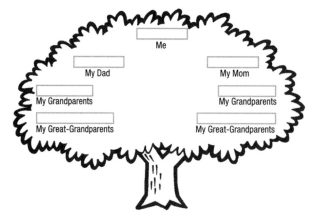

In the first chapter of the Book of Matthew, we find a listing of Jesus' family. Matthew shows Jesus is related to Abraham as well as King David. Jesus fulfilled God's promise to Abraham that "everyone would be blessed through him" (Genesis 12:3). In the same way, Jesus fulfilled God's promise to David recorded in 2 Samuel 7:16 that his kingdom would last forever.

Matthew also helps us understand that Jesus is not just a person related to people from long ago. Matthew helps us know Jesus is with us now.

Read Matthew 1:22-23.

- **What name did Matthew say would be given to the Son?**

- **What does *Immanuel* mean?**

- **How does it make you feel to know Jesus is with you?**

- **Read Matthew 28:19-20. How do these verses connect with Matthew 1:22-23?**

As disciples of Jesus, we believe His authority. And because we believe, we seek to obey His commands. In order to do that, we must depend on the presence of Jesus as we follow Him.

- **Reread Matthew 28:20. How long did Jesus say He would be with us?**

- **How does it make you feel to know Jesus will always be with you? Why?**

Read 1 Corinthians 12:7-11.

Paul wrote about the spiritual gifts people receive from God.

- **What is the purpose of spiritual gifts?**

- **Which gift(s) do you feel God has given you? Why?**

In 1 Corinthians 12:4-6, Paul made it clear that it is only through Jesus' presence that our spiritual gifts have value. We can accomplish nothing without Jesus' presence working in us. Jesus promised to remain with us through the amazing gift of the Holy Spirit! (Read John 14:16-18.)

- **As a follower of Jesus, in what ways do you rely on the Holy Spirit?**

- **What keeps you from relying more heavily on the Holy Spirit? What can you do to remove these obstacles?**

► THINK ABOUT THIS

When we walk in the presence of Jesus we are able to do more things than we could ever imagine. We have the opportunities to make disciples of Jesus. We have the privilege of inviting people to ask Jesus to be their Savior and Lord. This does not happen because of anything we do; instead it happens because of the work of the Holy Spirit.

- **How has the Holy Spirit worked in your life?**

God has promised us He will never leave us. He wants to work in and through us. Using the gifts He has given us, God will do amazing things if we allow Him to do so. Are you willing for God to work through you? If so, tell Him. If not, ask Him what needs to change in your life so you will be willing.

Throughout this study, I mentioned that our goal as followers of Jesus is to make disciples in all nations—that is our mission in the world. However, this raises another question—*How can we realistically spread the gospel to every people group?*

- **How would you respond to this question?**

When we think about it, the answer to this question is rather simple. Let's look at the life of Jesus. He spent His life investing in a few people. His plan for reaching all peoples was clear— make disciple-makers. If we follow Jesus' example, we can spend time helping other people become disciples of Jesus, then they find people to disciple, and those disciples disciple others.

Look at this graph. If I spent time discipling two people who then discipled two people, and this continued, look at how many people would be discipled.

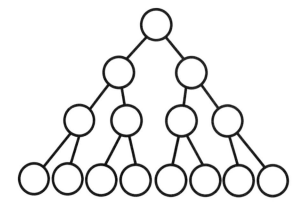

- **Write down the names of several people you know who are trying to live as disciples of Jesus.**

- **Which one of these people would be interested in meeting with you and growing as a follower of Jesus?**

Part of disciple-making includes teaching people to obey everything Jesus has commanded.

- **How well do you obey everything Jesus has commanded?**

- **How can you help your friends obey Jesus' commands?**

Review Matthew 4:18-22.

As followers of Jesus, we are also leaders. Jesus told the disciples He would make them "fishers of men." As "fishers," the disciples were to train the people who followed them, not as followers of the disciples, but as followers of Jesus.

Read Paul's words in 1 Corinthians 11:1 and Philippians 4:9. Paul lived his life in front of these believers so he could say, "Follow my example."

► THINK ABOUT THIS

- **Do your actions show that you are following Jesus? Why or why not?**

- **What impact would those actions have on people around you?**

- **What keeps you from sharing what you believe about Jesus with people around you?**

In order to effectively tell people how to study the Bible, you must first study the Bible yourself. In order to effectively tell people how to share what they believe, you must share what you believe first.

Your circumstances are different from my circumstances. I have already finished school, married, had children, and have a career. I know you are a preteen. You are wondering, *How can I do all of this? I don't even know how to study my Bible, so how can I help someone else?* You may just be starting the journey as a follower of Jesus. If that is so, I am so excited for you. I want to encourage you to talk with your Bible study leader or your pastor about how to study your Bible, pray, and share what you believe about Jesus. Please, do not wait until you think you know everything you need to before you begin telling people about Jesus.

Wherever you are on your path of following Jesus, please make it a priority to grow in your relationship with Him. The Bible promises God will give you everything you need to be used by Him.

Look back over your answers in today's study. Spend time reflecting on your journey as a follower of Jesus. Ask God to help you have a closer relationship with Him each day.

Look at the world map. Circle where you live. In what ways can you impact people in your city, state, country, and throughout the world?

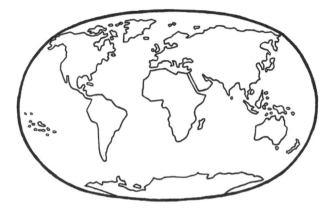

Yesterday we looked at the impact we can have by discipling a few people. Today, let's discover how we can impact every nation, tribe, language, and people in the world.

PRAYING FOR THE NATIONS

How many different countries are there in the world?

__ 50   __ 97   __ 152   __ 195   __ 295

Did you check 195? You and I have an opportunity to be a part of what God is doing around the world by praying for these countries. Let's pray for the people living in these countries to be open to hearing and responding to the gospel.

Look at a list of country names on a website. Write the names of five countries in the space. Pray for the people who live in these countries to hear about and respond to Jesus.

GIVING TO THE NATIONS

* **How do you feel about giving away things you own?**

Researchers estimate that Christians in North America give an average of 2.5% of their income to a local church.[1] (I think this is probably a generous estimate, but we will go with it.) These local churches then give an average of about 2 percent of these funds to the spread of the gospel overseas. In other words, for every $100 a person receives as income, only about $.05 is used to share the gospel in the rest of the world.

- **How does this information make you feel? Why?**

- **What percentage of your income (allowance, gifts, jobs) do you give?**

As a follower of Jesus, how will you sacrifice your wants in order to give to the needs of the world—most particularly the need for every people group to hear the gospel?

- **How willing are you to give sacrificially in order to help spread the gospel among all peoples?**

GOING TO THE NATIONS

- **If you could travel anywhere in the world, where would you go? Why would you want to visit that place?**

For centuries, people could only travel around the world by ship. In 1914, this changed with the beginning of commercial air travel. Today, people fly around the world in a matter of hours. Traveling to foreign countries is fairly easy. As people travel, they can tell others about the gospel and how it can change their lives.

Look at the kids in your school, neighborhood, or city. How many different nationalities are represented? You may never have to leave your city to tell people around the world about Jesus. As you tell the kids in your neighborhood about Jesus, they can then tell their family members and friends when they return to the countries they came from. As a result, you can tell people around the world.

- **In what other ways can you tell people around the world about Jesus?**

SEARCH THE SCRIPTURES

Read Acts 1:8.

We read this verse earlier in our study, but I think it best summarizes what we are learning about today. If we summarized this verse in just a few words it would say—You are a witness everywhere you go!

We are followers of Jesus. We have died to ourselves, and we know Jesus lives in us. He has saved us from our sins. He has transformed our minds with His truth, fulfilled our desires with His joy, and adapted our ways to His will.

He has joined us together in bodies of believers called the local churches for the accomplishment of one commission—to spread His gospel around the world.

This task involves all of us. Every child of God has been invited by God to be on His team. Every disciple of Jesus has been called, loved, created, and saved to make disciples of Jesus who make disciples of Jesus who make disciples of Jesus—until the grace of God is enjoyed and the glory of God is exalted among every people group in the world.

- **How committed are you to praying, giving, and going?**

Very committed   **Not committed**

Ask God to help you become more committed in praying, giving, and going so that all people of the world can hear and experience the gospel of Jesus.

[1]**Generous Giving, "Key Statistics on Generous Giving,"** *http://library.generousgiving.org/page. as;?sec=4$page=311.*

For the last six weeks we have examined what it means to be a disciple of Jesus. Let's spend today reflecting on what we discovered.

- **When did you decide to become a follower of Jesus?**

- **Why did you decide to become a follower of Jesus?**

- **How is your life different since becoming a follower of Jesus?**

- **In what ways are you helping other people become followers of Jesus?**

SEARCH THE SCRIPTURES

Read Acts 10:1-33. Simon Peter was a fisherman before Jesus called him to follow Him.

- **How did God use Simon Peter to spread the gospel around the world?**

THINK ABOUT THIS

Think about the disciples. In what ways did God use each of them to spread the gospel around the world? What about Paul, Timothy, and Aquila and Priscilla?

- **If someone wrote a book about your life, what would he say about you? Would he include any information about your being a follower of Jesus? What would he say you did to spread the gospel around the world?**

I am not sure where you are on the road to becoming a follower of Jesus. You may just be beginning, or you may have been on the road for a long time. My challenge is for you to continue growing closer to Jesus every day, and then find a friend to bring along with you. May God bless you as you follow His Son Jesus.

Supplies

- Index cards
- Markers
- Masking tape
- Large sheet of paper
- *Follow Me* Preteen Bible Study guides (1 per preteen)
- Pencils

Prep

- Make definition posters for *disciple, deny, repent, grace,* and *submission* (see pages 8, 11, 13, 17, 18).
- Prepare 10 "sin" cards (1 sin on each index card), such as *"white" lie, shoplifting, cheating on a test, killing someone, bullying someone, disobeying parents, saying God's name in an inappropriate way,* and so forth (1 set for each group of 3 to 4 preteens).

Introduce the Session

- Play "Twisted Follow the Leader!"
  - → Choose a volunteer to be the leader.
  - → Instruct the other preteens to be the followers.
  - → Explain: "The leader will move around the room doing actions for the others to follow. If a person does not copy the leader's motions, he is out of the game. We will continue until only one person is following the leader."
  - → Play the game.
  - → Select an adult leader to call out, "Come follow me!" and begin leading the preteens around the room.
  - → Observe how many preteens follow the teacher.
- Ask: "How did you decide whom to follow? When the teacher called out for you to follow her, did you respond immediately to her request, or did you hesitate, wondering whom to follow? Why?"
- Say: "Today we're going to begin a study of what it means to follow Jesus. Let's begin by reading how four men responded when Jesus called them to follow Him."

Search the Scriptures

- Invite a preteen to read aloud Matthew 4:18-22.
- Ask: "Why did Simon Peter, Andrew, James, and John respond immediately to Jesus' invitation to follow Him?"
- Continue: "What did these men give up to follow Jesus?"
- Explain: "Jesus eventually chose 12 men to be His disciples. Can you name all 12 of the disciples?"
- Write the disciples' names on the paper.

- Guide the preteens to locate Matthew 10:2-4 to verify the names.
- Ask: "What does the word *disciple* mean?"
- Display the *disciple* definition.
- Invite a volunteer to read aloud the definition.
- Ask: "What do you think it means to be a disciple of Jesus? How would you respond to someone who asked you how he can become a follower of Jesus?"
- Allow the preteens to explain what they would say to someone about becoming a Christian.
- Select volunteers to read aloud John 3:1-21.
- Discuss the questions Nicodemus asked and how Jesus responded.
- Ask: "How is *being born again* like *dying to yourself*?"
- Distribute *Follow Me* Preteen Bible Study guides and pencils.
- Guide the preteens to locate page 9 in their guides.
- Invite a volunteer to read aloud the third paragraph ("To die to yourself means …").
- Call on a preteen to read aloud Matthew 16:24.
- Explain: "When we die to ourselves, we deny *[display poster]* what we want and we choose to do whatever Jesus wants us to do. When a person becomes a Christian, her life should reflect her relationship of following Jesus."
- Continue: "So how does a person become a Christian?"
- Lead each preteen to select a partner.
- Say: "Locate 'God's Plan' on pages 23-24. Read the information and practice telling each other how to become a Christian."
- Display *repent* poster to one preteen.
- Say: "Without saying anything, act out the definition of the word. Let's see if anyone can guess the word."
- Allow the preteens to call out words as the volunteer acts out the definition.
- Display the poster to the entire group.
- Say: "We can only be saved by repenting—turning from our sin and ourselves, and turning toward Jesus."
- Select volunteers to read aloud Galatians 4:4-5 and Ephesians 1:5.
- Ask: "What do these verses tell us about our relationship with God?"
- Say: "God uses the picture of adoption to describe His relationship with people when they become Christians. When we become Christians, we are adopted into God's family."
- Invite preteens to describe adoption situations.
- Relate the stories to being adopted into God's family.
- Form groups of three to four preteens.
- Provide each group with a set of "sin" cards.
- Explain: "Arrange the cards from the least to the worst sin."
- Compare the groups' arrangements.
- Ask: "How did you decide the order of the sins?"
- Read aloud Romans 3:23 and Romans 6:23.
- Inquire: "What do these verses tell us about sin?"

- Say: "In God's eyes, a sin is a sin. God does not rank sins from least to worst. Everything we do that is opposite of what He wants us to do is a sin. The Bible says that the punishment for sin is death."
- Explain: "Because we all sin, none of us *deserve* to have a relationship with God. However, God *wants* to have a relationship with us. That's where grace impacts our lives."
- Display *grace* definition poster.
- Select a volunteer to read aloud John 15:16.
- Continue: "Although we don't deserve to have a relationship with God, Jesus has invited us to follow Him. Through His death, burial, and resurrection, Jesus made it possible for us to have this relationship."
- Ask: "What was the last invitation you received to do something? How did you respond to the invitation?"
- Continue: "How did Simon Peter, Andrew, James, and John respond to Jesus' invitation to follow Him?"
- Say: "When we choose to follow Jesus, we are to be fully committed to Him."
- Call attention to the commitment scales on pages 18-19.
- Guide the preteens to indicate how committed they are to these areas of their lives.
- Ask: "What is the difference between being committed to church and being committed to Jesus? Can you be committed to the church without being committed to Jesus? Can you be committed to Jesus without being committed to the church?"
- Read aloud John 3:16.
- Say: "God demonstrated how much He loves us when He sent Jesus to die on the cross and endure God's wrath (punishment) so that we can have a relationship with Him. Because of Jesus' grace, mercy, and love demonstrated on the cross, we are invited to follow Him. He deserves nothing less than total commitment."
- Encourage the preteens to discuss what changes they need to make to be fully committed to Jesus.
- Ask: "How do actions help us know about a person's character? How do people know if we are followers of Jesus?"
- Recall Jesus' conversation with Nicodemus.
- Say: "During their discussion, Jesus recalled words from the Old Testament prophet, Ezekiel, when Jesus told Nicodemus that God would give people a new heart and cleanse them from sin—God would change their lives! God wants to change our lives, too!"
- Invite preteens to read aloud things that happen when a person comes to Jesus (page 22).

Think About This

- Say: "Jesus has a purpose for our lives. He is inviting us to join Him in fulfilling that purpose. He is inviting us just as He invited Simon Peter, Andrew, James, and John to follow Him."
- State: "I know some of you may not have trusted Jesus to be your Savior and Lord yet. If you would like to talk about this, I will be glad to talk with you."

- Encourage preteens who are Christians to thank God for the gift of salvation He has given them.
- Challenge preteens to think about:
    → In what ways is Jesus changing your life so you can be His disciple?
    → Is there anything in your life you are not willing to give up to follow Jesus?
- Pray, asking God to help the preteens be willing to do whatever is needed to be fully committed to following Jesus.

Overview the Week

- Explain: "This week you will dig deeper into what we talked about today. Start on page 7 of your study guide. Read the information, reflect on the questions, and write down your answers. Review the activities we completed in class. Each day should take you 20-25 minutes to complete. Do not rush through the Bible studies. Allow God to speak to you as you study and apply these teachings to your life."

Week 2
Teaching Plan

Supplies

- Modeling clay
- Large sheets of paper
- Markers
- Masking tape
- Non-poisonous houseplant with long vines
- Pencils
- *Follow Me* Preteen Bible Study guides (1 per preteen)
- Construction paper
- Scissors
- Index cards
- Poster board

Prep

- Make definition posters for *transformation, desire, favoritism, purpose,* and *abide* (see pages 25, 31, 34, 36, 38).
- Display the plant.
- Attach a large sheet of paper in a vertical position to a focal wall. Draw or cut out and attach a large vine through the middle of the paper.
- Prepare assignment cards. On index cards, write ways to stay connected to Jesus (1 method per card): *Read and study your Bible; Pray; Worship God; Tell people what you believe; Ask someone to keep you accountable.*
- Cut out fruit shapes from construction paper (5 per preteen).

Introduce the Session

- Provide each preteen a ball of modeling clay.
- Instruct preteens to shape the clay to resemble a person, animal, or other object.
- Allow children to tell about their designs.
- Say: "You changed the clay's shape and appearance by molding and shaping it. What's a word that means 'to change completely'?"
- Allow responses.
- Display the *transformation* poster.
- Say: "Last week we learned what it means to be a follower of Jesus. What are some things you discovered in your daily Bible study times?"
- Continue: "This week we will learn some of the areas of our lives Jesus wants to transform. He wants to transform us—change us—into what He wants us to be."
- Pray.

Search the Scriptures

- Distribute construction paper and scissors.
- Guide: "Everyone cut out a branch from construction paper to attach to the vine. Write your name on your branch, then attach it to the vine."
- Assist as needed.
- Read aloud John 15:1-5.
- Ask: "In the illustration we just read, who is the vine?"
- Label the vine *Jesus*.
- Call attention to the houseplant. Break off one of the leaves/branches.
- Ask: "What happens when a branch is no longer connected to the vine?"
- Affirm: "When a branch is no longer connected to the vine, the branch will die because it cannot receive the necessary nutrients. A dead branch cannot produce fruit."
- Ask: "Why is it important that we stay connected to Jesus?"
- Explain: "When we stay connected to Jesus (the Vine), He transforms us into what He wants us to become."
- Inquire: "What are some changes that have happened to you in the last year?" (*grew taller, made new friends, learned new things in school, etc.*)
- Call attention to changes related to being connected to Jesus.
- Say: "Let's discover ways we can stay connected to Jesus."
- Form five teams.
- Distribute poster board, markers, and one assignment card to each team.
- Say: "Let's discover five ways we can be transformed. Each team has a card. Design a poster to communicate the method written on your card. Be creative."
- Assist as needed.
- Invite each team to display and tell about the poster.
- Discuss the benefits of each method.
- Say: "These methods are ways we stay connected to Jesus. The better connected we are to Jesus, the more we can be transformed into the followers He desires."
- Select volunteers to read aloud Matthew 22:37; Romans 8:5-7; and Colossians 3:2.
- Ask: "What do these verses tell us about our minds?"

- State: "Jesus wants to change our minds so we think more like Him."
- Read aloud Romans 12:1-2.
- Point out that when Jesus controls our thoughts, we stop following the sinful ways of the world.
- Display the *desire* poster.
- Enlist a volunteer to read aloud the definition.
- Ask: "What are some things you desire? How do your desires impact the way you live? How would you feel if Jesus asked you to give up everything you own to follow Him?"
- Explain: "To be followers of Jesus we must be willing to give up everything."
- Ask: "How do you like to be treated? Do people always treat one another in kind ways? What are some other ways people treat one another?"
- Write the actions on a large sheet of paper.
- Say: "When we begin to think like Jesus and want the same things He wants, we will start acting like Him as well."
- Invite the preteens to circle the actions that show how Jesus treated people (page 33).
- Display *favoritism* poster.
- Read aloud the definition.
- Ask: "Did Jesus ever show favoritism to anyone?"
- Say: "Jesus treated everyone the same way—with respect."
- Select a preteen to read aloud John 15:12-15.
- Ask: "How can we help people realize they are important and that God loves them?"
- Display *purpose* poster.
- Read aloud the definition.
- Say: "When we become followers of Jesus, we commit to doing what He wants us to do instead of what we want to do. Jesus has a purpose for us—to 'bear fruit.'"
- Call on a preteen to read aloud John 15:5.
- Continue: "Every day we come in contact with people who need to hear about Jesus."
- Distribute fruit shapes and markers.
- Lead the preteens to write on the shapes initials of people they know who are not Christians.
- Guide the preteens to attach their shapes to the branches of the vine.
- Ask: "According to John 15:5, what must take place for us to produce fruit?"
- Continue: "What does it mean to *abide* in Jesus? How does Jesus abide in His followers?"
- Display *abide* poster.
- Read aloud the definition.
- Select a volunteer to read aloud John 15:5-10.
- Ask: "What is the result of abiding in Jesus?"
- Point out that the Holy Spirit's presence in our lives gives us strength to live in ways that please and honor God.

Apply the Truths

- Ask: "What will you say if your parents ask you, 'What did you learn today?'"
- Allow the preteens to review what they learned.
- Ask: "Why is it important for a branch to be attached to a vine? How does this metaphor apply to us? Why must we remain attached to Jesus, the Vine? What happens when we are not attached to Him?"
- Continue: "We must let God change us—transform us—in order to follow Jesus."
- Challenge the preteens to reflect on these questions: *Are you attached to the Vine? If not, why not? If yes, how are you growing? What areas of your life need to be changed? What are you willing to give up to follow Jesus?*
- Guide the preteens to bow their heads and close their eyes.
- Read aloud the following prayer topics, pausing after each one to allow time for the preteens to silently voice prayers.
  - → Ask God to help you stay attached to Jesus.
  - → Ask God to help you allow Him to transform you into the follower of Jesus He wants you to be.
  - → Confess any times you have not been willing to be transformed.
  - → Thank God for everything He has given you. Ask Him to help you to be willing to give these things up to follow Jesus.
  - → Ask God to help you live in ways that tell people they are important and that God loves them.
  - → Pray for opportunities to bear fruit by telling people about Jesus.
  - → Ask God to help you follow Jesus, abide in Him, and make disciples.
- Pray for each preteen by name, asking God to help the preteens allow Him to change them into what He wants them to be.

Week 3
Teaching Plan

Supplies

- Paper
- Pencils
- Markers
- Large sheets of paper
- Container
- Index cards
- Stopwatch or watch with second hand
- *Follow Me* Preteen Bible Study guides (1 per preteen)

- Make definition posters for *adopt, love, need, want, pleasures, pursuits, possessions, worship, delight,* and *fast* (see pages 41, 42, 45, 49, 53, 56).
- Write chores (*feed dog, sweep floor, mow yard, fold clothes,* etc.) on index cards (1 chore per card). Place in the container.
- Prepare "Spiritual Growth" assignments (1 group assignment on each index card).

Group 1: Read the Bible

→ Read Psalm 19:7-11.
→ Answer these questions:
  → What do these verses tell you about reading and studying the Bible?
  → Why is it important to read and study the Bible?

Group 2: Pray

→ Read Matthew 6:6.
→ Answer these questions:
  → Why is prayer important?
  → What can we do to have a better prayer time?

Group 3: Worship

→ Read Acts 16:25-34, and the definitions of *worship* and *delight*. (See posters.)
→ Answer these questions:
  → Why do we worship God?
  → What are some ways we can worship God and delight in Him?

Group 4: Fast

→ Read Matthew 6:16-18, and the definition of *fast*. (See posters.)
→ Answer these questions:
  → What is fasting?
  → What guidelines did Jesus give the disciples for fasting?

Group 5: Give

→ Read Matthew 6:19-24.
→ Answer these questions:
  → Why is it important to give?
  → What does our giving indicate about our priorities?

Introduce the Session

- Distribute paper, pencils, and markers.
- Challenge preteens to draw a picture or write songs about their families.
- Allow preteens to tell about their families by showing their pictures or reading aloud their songs.
- Remind preteens that last week they learned about some of the areas God wants to transform so we can fulfill the purpose He has for us.

- Encourage preteens to state what they discovered by working through the sessions.
- Say: "Today we will talk about what it means to be a part of God's family."

Search the Scriptures

- Ask: "What comes to mind when you hear the word *adopt*?"
- Display the *adopt* poster.
- Ask: "Do you know anyone who was adopted? How has being adopted changed the person's life?"
- Allow preteens to respond.
- Guide preteens to stand in various locations around the room.
- Explain: "I will start a sentence. I want you to shout out an answer, then find someone who is shouting out the same item as you and stand together."
- Read aloud statements, such as, "I love my …; I love eating …; I love watching …" and so forth.
- Identify how preteens responded after each statement.
- Guide preteens back to their seats.
- Ask: "How do you define *love*? What's the difference between the way we love our dogs, love eating pizza, or love watching a certain TV show, and the way we love God?"
- Display *love* poster.
- Select a volunteer to read aloud the definition.
- Invite a preteen to read aloud 1 John 3:1.
- Explain: "God loves us so much that He provided a way for us to be adopted into His family. When we are adopted into God's family, we can call Him *Father*."
- Continue: "A responsibility of a father is to provide the things his children need. Let's make a list of things we need."
- Write items on paper as preteens name them.
- Display *need* and *want* posters.
- Select volunteers to read aloud the definitions.
- Say: "Examine the list of things we made. As a group, let's determine which things are needs and which ones are wants."
- Write *W* beside wants, and *N* beside needs as the preteens indicate the differences.
- Say: "When we are adopted into God's family, we can trust Him to provide for our needs."
- Form two groups.
- Guide one group to locate Exodus 16 in their Bibles while the other group locates John 6.
- Say: "Examine the chapters to discover how God provided for the people's needs."
- Assist as needed.
- Invite both groups to report their findings.
- Ask: "How do you think our wants change when we are adopted into God's family?"
- Discuss the preteens responses.
- Explain: "When we are adopted into God's family, we should want the same things He wants."
- Guide each preteen to select a partner.

- Say: "Each of you will have 30 seconds to tell about things that make you happy. Select a person to begin."
- Inform the preteens to begin. Call time after 30 seconds and repeat.
- Read aloud John 10:10.
- Ask: "What did Jesus say was His purpose in coming to earth? What does it mean to *have life*? Did Jesus mean He would give us everything we want?"
- Display and read aloud *pleasures*, *pursuits*, and *possessions* definitions.
- Explain: "When we follow Jesus, we find our happiness in Him. We give up wanting 'things' we think will bring us happiness and discover Jesus meets our needs. Our ultimate happiness is not found in things we want, have, or enjoy, but in Jesus!"
- Place the container in front of the group.
- Select a volunteer to choose a card and act out the action.
- Allow preteens to guess the action.
- Continue with additional cards.
- Ask: "What do all of these actions have in common?"
- Explain: "These are chores we do at home. Do you enjoy doing chores? Why or why not?"
- Continue: "Most of the time we do not enjoy doing our chores. However, if we don't do them, our homes can become unhealthy."
- Ask: "What are some things followers of Jesus do that can become 'chores'?"
- Record the actions on the paper.
- State: "We have a number of things we can do to grow closer to God, but we should want to do these things instead of thinking of them as 'chores.'"
- Form five groups.
- Distribute a "Spiritual Growth" card to each group.
- Guide the groups to complete their assignments.
- Invite each group to tell about the findings.
- Say: "These are just some ways we can grow in our relationship with Jesus. We can also grow as we tell people about Jesus and deal with challenges in our lives."

Apply the Truths

- Ask: "Do you enjoy being a part of God's family? Why or why not?"
- Continue: "How are our lives different from people who are not a part of God's family?"
- Compare and contrast the lives of Christians with non-Christians.
- Challenge preteens to commit to growing in their relationships with God by reading the Bible, praying, worshiping, fasting, giving, and telling people about Jesus.
- Pray, thanking God for adopting people into His family. Ask God to help the preteens focus on happiness in Jesus rather than in things. Ask God to help the preteens have an attitude of "get to" instead of "have to" about doing things to grow closer to Him.

Supplies

- Unfamiliar household objects/tools
- Paper
- Pencils
- World map
- *Follow Me* Preteen Bible Study guides (1 per preteen)
- Index cards
- Marker
- Masking tape

Prep

- Make definition posters for *redeem, commission,* and *empower* (see pages 66, 69, 70).
- Number and display unfamiliar/unusual household items/tools around the room.
- Display the world map on a focal wall.

Introduce the Session

- Distribute index cards and pencils.
- Allow pairs of preteens to work together to identify the purposes of the items by writing their guesses on index cards.
- Invite preteens to read aloud their guesses, then reveal the purposes of the items.
- Congratulate preteens for their efforts.
- Say: "Last week we learned what it means to be a part of God's family. What are some things you discovered in your daily Bible study times?"
- Continue: "This week we will learn what our purpose is as a member of God's family. Just as each of the items has a purpose, God has a purpose for our lives."

Search the Scriptures

- Select a preteen to read aloud Matthew 4:19.
- Ask: "What does it mean to be a 'fisher of men'? Where are we supposed to 'fish for men'?"
- Read aloud Acts 1:8.
- Guide preteens to fill in the blanks on page 59 as they think about their "Jerusalem," "Judea," and "Samaria."
- Say: "Jesus expects us to be a witness for Him no matter where we go!"
- Instruct preteens to stand together in the center of the room.
- Say: "I will call out two words in a category. You must choose which of the two you like best and form a group with the other preteens choosing the same thing."
- Call out pairs of words, such as chocolate/vanilla, red/blue, winter/summer, pizza/hamburgers, and so forth.

- Ask: "Knowing which of the two things you liked best probably wasn't too difficult, but how do we know God's will or purpose for our lives—what He wants us to do?"
- Allow discussion.
- Invite a preteen to read aloud Luke 9:23.
- Continue: "Jesus was fully dedicated to doing God's will. Jesus expects us to do the same by being willing to give up everything to follow Him."
- Encourage preteens to state ways Jesus impacted (affected/changed) the lives of people as He was doing God's will.
- Say: "Sometimes Jesus did things Himself and other times He chose to work through people. Jesus wants to use His followers to impact the world."
- Ask: "What are some ways we impact others? In what ways can we impact people in negative ways? In positive ways?"
- Say: "Good news! God doesn't expect us to be perfect before He can use us to impact the world for Him! All we need to do is choose to allow Him to use us."
- Call attention to the world map.
- Ask: "What is God's will for the world?"
- Invite two volunteers to read aloud Matthew 28:19-20 and Acts 1:7-8.
- Continue: "What do these verses say about God's will for the world?"
- Display and read aloud the *redeem* definition.
- Say: "God's will is for everyone from every nation, tribe, language, and people to be redeemed through His grace and for His glory."
- Ask: "What role do Jesus' followers play in spreading His kingdom in the world?"
- Say: "Our purpose—God's will for us—is to make disciples."
- Continue: "How does it make you feel to know Jesus wants you to make disciples by telling people about Him and helping them grow in their relationship with Him?"
- Display and read aloud the *commission* definition.
- Reread Matthew 28:19-20.
- Explain: "These verses are often called 'The Great Commission' because Jesus instructed (commissioned) His disciples to go into all the world and tell people about Him. How does God help us tell people around the world about Jesus?"
- Select a preteen to reread Acts 1:7-8.
- Display and read aloud the *empower* definition.
- Explain: "In order for us to make disciples, we must be empowered by the Holy Spirit. We receive the Holy Spirit when we become Christians. The presence of the Holy Spirit in our lives enables us to tell people about Jesus."
- Guide the preteens to open their *Follow Me* study guides to page 73.
- Direct: "Write down names of people you know who are not Christians."
- Say: "Let's pray for these people right now."
- Pray, asking God to help the people listed to know how much He loves them.
- Ask: "What fears keep people from telling others about Jesus?"
- Explain: "As followers of Jesus, He lives in us and has given us the Holy Spirit to help us, so we can trust that He will help us overcome our fear."
- Invite a preteen to pray that God will give everyone courage to tell people about Jesus.
- Guide each preteen to select a partner.

- Say: "Talk about all the places you will go and the people you will see this week."
- Remind: "God expects us to be witnesses everywhere we go!"
- Direct partners to pray asking God to help them recognize opportunities to tell people about Jesus wherever they go.
- Read aloud Acts 4:1-12.
- Ask: "What happened as a result of Peter and John's willingness to tell people what they believed about Jesus? By whose power did Peter and John say they taught?"
- State: "God's purpose for us is to tell people about Jesus. He has given us the Holy Spirit to help us."

Apply the Truths

- Say: "The more we tell people about Jesus, the easier it becomes. Let's take time to practice telling people about Jesus."
- Guide preteens back to their partners.
- Instruct: "Pretend one of you is not a Christian. Your partner will tell you about his relationship with Jesus and how you can become a follower of Jesus. Ask questions and role-play the situation."
- Observe the preteens.
- Point out your observations.
- Challenge preteens to tell someone about Jesus this week and to complete the chart about their experience (page 76).
- Pray, thanking God for the opportunities to tell people about Jesus.

Week 5
Teaching Plan

Supplies

- Poster board or large sheets of paper
- Markers
- Tape
- Index cards
- Paper
- Container
- *Follow Me* Preteen Bible Study guides (1 per preteen)

Prep

- Make definition posters for *church, discipline,* and *service* (see pages 77, 83, 90).
- Write team assignments on index cards (1 assignment per card):
  *Team 1—1 Corinthians 12:4-11; Team 2—1 Corinthians 12:12-26;
  Team 3—1 Corinthians 12:27-31.*

Introduce the Session

- Form teams of three or four preteens.
- Distribute paper and markers.
- Guide teams to draw pictures of a church.
- Attach the pictures to the focal wall.
- Display and discuss *church* definitions.
- Compare drawings to the definitions.
- Say: "Last week we learned about God's will for our lives. What are some things you discovered in your daily Bible study times?"
- Continue: "This week we will discover what it means for a follower of Jesus to be a part of His church."

Search the Scriptures

- Ask: "Do you agree or disagree with this statement: 'It is impossible to make a commitment to Jesus without making a commitment to the church'?"
- Invite preteens who agree with the statement to stand. Allow them to tell why they agree with the statement.
- Instruct preteens who disagree with the statement to stand and explain why they disagree.
- Read aloud Hebrews 10:24-25.
- Ask: "What do these verses tell us to do?"
- State: "When you trust Jesus as your Savior and Lord, you commit your life to His church."
- State: "Let's discover the importance of working together. Everyone stand as close together as we can. Reach across the group and hold someone's right hand. Now hold someone else's left hand. Our goal is to untangle the web without letting go of the hands we are holding."
- Guide the preteens to work together to untangle the web.
- Ask: "Was this easy? Why? When you saw how to untangle the web, did you help someone? How did we work together?"
- Say: "Throughout the New Testament, the church is described as the body of Christ. Followers of Jesus are parts of the body. We each have a function in the body—the church. Let's explore these functions."
- Form three teams.
- Distribute team assignment cards.
- Instruct each team to read the assigned verses, noting the main points in the passages.
- Assist as needed.
- Invite one person from each team to report on the main points of the passages.
- Ask: "In what ways does the church function as a team? What happens when people do not fulfill their purpose in the church?"
- Say: "In order for the church to be what God wants it to be, we each must play our part in the body."
- Talk about various ways preteens can serve in the church.
- Challenge each preteen to find a way to serve.

- Ask: "What do you think of when you hear the word *discipline*?"
- Compare and contrast the preteens' thoughts.
- Display and read aloud the *discipline* definition.
- Ask: "What kind of discipline does a person need to be a good athlete? A good student? A follower of Jesus?"
- Invite a preteen to read aloud Matthew 18:15-20.
- Explain: "Jesus wants His followers to be committed to Him. When people are not living in ways that please and honor Him, we should lovingly talk with them."
- Ask: "Why do you think these verses instruct us to talk with someone in private before involving others?"
- Continue: "A WORD OF WARNING: We must be willing to examine our lives and change what needs to be changed before pointing out things other people are doing wrong!"
- Read aloud Acts 2:37-47.
- Discuss things the believers did after responding to Peter's teaching *(met together, ate together, shared everything they owned, praised God)*.
- Ask: "How do the actions of the early church compare to what our church does? Why do you think it's important for followers of Jesus to spend time with other followers? What does it mean to be a member of a local church?"
- Explain: "As members of a church, we not only belong to Jesus, we belong to each other. We all have different backgrounds, different personalities, different likes and dislikes, but we all form one church—connected by our relationship with Jesus."
- Select a preteen to read aloud Ephesians 4:11-13.
- Ask: "What responsibilities did God give people? What is the purpose of these responsibilities?"
- Invite preteens to identify people in your church who fulfill these responsibilities.
- Read aloud John 13:35.
- Continue: "According to John 13:35, how are we, as followers of Jesus, to respond to one another?"
- Lead preteens to take two minutes to list ways people serve in your church (page 90).
- Allow preteens to compare their lists.
- Display and read aloud the *service* definition.
- Distribute index cards.
- Instruct: "Without letting anyone see your answer, write one way you can serve in our church."
- Collect the cards and place in a container.
- Call on a volunteer to choose a card and to pantomime as the preteens attempt to guess the action.
- Continue with the additional cards.
- Review the opportunities preteens can serve.
- Invite preteens to tell about ways they currently serve in the church.

Apply the Truths

- Read aloud John 13:1-11.
- Ask: "In what way did Jesus serve the disciples? Why do you think Jesus served the disciples in this way?"
- Say: "Jesus wanted to show His followers what it means to serve others. He demonstrated that we should be willing to do whatever needs to be done."
- Continue: "Being a member of a local church is very important. We have all been given gifts to use to serve God."
- Challenge preteens to think about how they would answer the following questions:
  - → How involved are you in your church?
  - → What is your role in the body of Christ?
  - → Are you serving other people in love?
- Pray. Thank God for your church and for its leadership. Ask God to help preteens be willing to serve.

Week 6
Teaching Plan

Supplies

- Balloons (3 different colors)
- Strips of paper
- Markers
- Poster board
- World map
- Masking tape
- Paper
- *Follow Me* Preteen Bible Study guides (1 per preteen)

Prep

- Make definition posters for *authority* and *spiritual gifts* (see pages 94, 101).
- Write the words of Matthew 28:18 on strips of paper (1 word per strip). Place the words in the same color of balloons (1 word per balloon). Repeat for verses 19 and 20 (1 color balloon per verse).
- Display the world map on a focal wall.
- Prepare *Pray, Give, Go* signs (1 word per sign). Attach to a focal wall.

Introduce the Session

- Say: "Last week we learned what it means for a follower of Jesus to serve in the church. What are some things you discovered in your daily Bible times?"
- Encourage preteens to tell about things they learned during the study.
- Form three teams. Assign each team a balloon color.

- Place the balloons around the room.
- Say: "Your mission is to work with your team members to collect and pop your assigned balloons, then gather the words inside the balloons. When you have all the words, locate Matthew 28:18-20 in your Bible. Finally, put your words in the correct order of the verse."
- Lead a volunteer from each team to read aloud the verse, starting with verse 18.
- Ask: "Who remembers what we usually call these verses? Why are they called 'The Great Commission'? This week we will finish our study by looking at our mission as followers of Jesus."

Search the Scriptures

- Invite a preteen to read aloud Matthew 28:18-20.
- Ask: "What commands did Jesus give His disciples?"
- Display and read aloud the *authority* definition.
- Ask: "Who has authority over you? How do you respond to people who have authority over you? How should you respond to people who have authority over you?"
- Say: "In verse 18, Jesus told His disciples that He had been given all authority in heaven and earth. How did Jesus demonstrate that authority while He was on earth?"
- Assign three volunteers to read aloud: Matthew 8:23-27; 9:1-8; 28:1-10.
- Affirm that Jesus demonstrated authority over the winds and sea, to forgive sins, and over death.
- Continue: "To be a *disciple of Jesus* means we live under His authority—we surrender every part of our lives to Him."
- Recall Matthew 28:19-20.
- Ask: "Are these verses a suggestion, a request, or a command?"
- Continue: "Jesus commanded His followers to make disciples by going, telling, and teaching other people about Him. Why should we tell other people about Jesus?" *(because God loves everyone and wants everyone to receive His gift of salvation; because Jesus is worthy of honor, glory, and praise)*
- Form three teams.
- Distribute poster board and markers.
- Assign each team one part of the command—Go, Tell, or Teach.
- Instruct each team to create a poster related to the assigned aspect of the command. (Refer preteens to pages 98-99 for ideas to include on the posters.)
- Invite teams to display and explain their posters.
- Say: "For us to be followers of Jesus, we must make disciples!"
- Display and read aloud the *spiritual gifts* definition.
- Explain: "Paul wrote about spiritual gifts people receive from God."
- Select a volunteer to read aloud 1 Corinthians 12:7-11.
- Encourage preteens to identify the spiritual gifts named in the passage.
- Ask: "Which gift(s) do you think God has given you?"
- Call attention to the *spiritual gifts* definition again.
- Affirm: "God gives spiritual gifts so they can be used by Christians to serve Him through churches."
- Read aloud 1 Corinthians 12:4-6.

- Ask: "What role does the Holy Spirit play in God working through us?"
- Say: "We cannot accomplish our mission of telling other people about Jesus without the Holy Spirit working in us."
- Guide preteens to find a partner and stand facing each other, about an arm's length apart.
- Appoint the preteen whose birthday comes earliest in the year to be the leader and his partner to be the follower.
- Instruct the follower to mirror/imitate the leader's movements and facial expressions.
- Switch roles and repeat the game.
- Call on volunteers to read aloud 1 Corinthians 11:1 and Philippians 4:9.
- Ask: "How do these verses relate to our game of imitating each other? Why is it important that our actions show we are following Jesus?"
- Say: "As followers of Jesus we are also leaders. We must be an example for others of what it looks like to follow Jesus."
- Call attention to the world map.
- Read aloud Acts 1:8.
- State: "Earlier in our study (Week 4) we discussed what our 'Jerusalems,' 'Judeas,' and 'Samarias' are—our city, state, and country. We talked about being examples for people around us, but what are some ways we can impact every nation, tribe, language, and people in the world?"
- Direct attention to the *Pray*, *Give*, and *Go* signs.
- Say: "We can pray, we can give, and we can go."
- Invite each preteen to select five countries on the world map.
- Say: "Write these names in the space on page 104 of your *Follow Me* study guide."
- Continue: "Ask God to help people living in these countries to be open to hearing and responding to the gospel."
- Ask: "How can preteens give sacrificially in order to help spread the gospel among all peoples?"
- Challenge preteens to think about what they will be willing to sacrifice to help people around the world hear the gospel.
- Ask: "How many nationalities are represented in your school, neighborhood, or city? How can sharing the gospel with people from other countries who live near you be like 'going' around the world?"
- Read aloud Acts 1:8 again.
- Say: "Our mission is to be witnesses everywhere we go!"

Apply the Truths

- Challenge preteens to complete the daily Bible study times this week.
- Encourage the preteens to continue growing closer to Jesus every day, and then to invite a friend to come along with them!
- Call attention to the four reflection questions (page 107). Encourage preteens to take time to evaluate their relationships with Jesus and to make necessary changes to be the followers of Jesus He desires.
- Pray for each preteen by name. Ask God to help the preteens—and you—to do whatever is needed to be followers of Jesus—fully committed to Him.